Tidbits and Pearls

Ladonna Shanks

*A Book of Essays on
Living Everyday Life with God*

*Barbara —
Blessings on you
as you continue in
your own spiritual quest.*

Ladonna Shanks

WESTBOW PRESS®
A DIVISION OF THOMAS NELSON
& ZONDERVAN

Copyright © 2019 Ladonna Shanks.

Janie Bell Oviatt, chapter title page and cover page artwork
Michele Bunch, photographer
You are free to contact the author at shankstidbits@gmail.com.

All rights reserved. No part of this book may be used or reproduced by any means, graphic, electronic, or mechanical, including photocopying, recording, taping or by any information storage retrieval system without the written permission of the author except in the case of brief quotations embodied in critical articles and reviews.

This book is a work of non-fiction. Unless otherwise noted, the author and the publisher make no explicit guarantees as to the accuracy of the information contained in this book.

WestBow Press books may be ordered through booksellers or by contacting:

WestBow Press
A Division of Thomas Nelson & Zondervan
1663 Liberty Drive
Bloomington, IN 47403
www.westbowpress.com
1 (866) 928-1240

Because of the dynamic nature of the Internet, any web addresses or links contained in this book may have changed since publication and may no longer be valid. The views expressed in this work are solely those of the author and do not necessarily reflect the views of the publisher, and the publisher hereby disclaims any responsibility for them.

ISBN: 978-1-9736-5858-0 (sc)
ISBN: 978-1-9736-5859-7 (hc)
ISBN: 978-1-9736-5857-3 (e)

Library of Congress Control Number: 2019904157

Print information available on the last page.

WestBow Press rev. date: 05/15/2019

Unless otherwise stated, definitions are taken from *Wiktionary*, https://en.wiktionary.org/wiki/Wiktionary:Main_Page.

Definition marked *Cambridge Dictionary* is from https://dictionary.cambridge.org/dictionary/.

Scripture quotations are from the New Revised Standard Version Bible, copyright © 1989 the Division of Christian Education of the National Council of the Churches of Christ in the United States of America. Used by permission. All rights reserved.

Scripture quotations marked KJV are taken from the King James Version of the Bible.

Scripture quotations marked NLT are taken from the *Holy Bible, New Living Translation*, copyright ©1996, 2004, 2015 by Tyndale House Foundation. Used by permission of Tyndale House Publishers, Inc., Carol Stream, Illinois 60188. All rights reserved.

Information about Yo-Yo Ma is taken from https://biography.yourdictionary.com/yo-yo-ma.

The Great Collaboration

collaboration: n. Joint production or creation.

Humans and God—a most unlikely combination of partners in a work of collaboration. And yet that is His idea, His plan. Created to have a friendship and a relationship with God, it is His desire that we live our lives with Him as He lives through us. That *is* the definition of living life and living it well.

How does one live life with God, the omnipotent, omniscient Creator of all? The one basic requisite is that of honesty—being honest with oneself and honest before Him.

I am His instrument, and without Him I can do nothing.

Contents

Introduction xi

Chapter 1   Family 1
Chapter 2   Gifts, Treasures, and Blessings 45
Chapter 3   In the Garden 69
Chapter 4   An Ordinary Life Extraordinaire 109
Chapter 5   Aging, Death, and Eternity 153

Introduction

In July, 1958, as a thirteen-year-old girl, I attended church camp at the idyllic Silver Falls State Park near Silverton, Oregon. It was my summer vacation, the one week when I took a break from fieldwork where I picked strawberries, raspberries, and beans for local farmers.

At the nightly chapel service, this entreaty was given: "Then I heard the voice of the Lord saying, 'Whom shall I send, and who will go for us?'" (Isaiah 6:8). My response, though filled with fear and trepidation, is as fresh in my memory as though it happened yesterday: "Here am I. Send me."

As a young girl, the base of my fear was that God would send me as a missionary overseas to some country—any country—where there were snakes. *That* He did not do.

I married and became a wife and then a mother. It was at that time He issued this charge: "All I have asked you to do is live your life." Silently, I nodded my head in assent as though I understood exactly what was meant. Even though I was an adult by then, nothing could have been further from the truth.

God desires to have a friendship, a relationship with those He created. He wants us to have rich, fulfilled lives, and He wants to be a part of that. He longs to share Himself with us, for us to share our lives and ourselves with Him. It is our choice to include Him or exclude Him. The very work of Christ as Redeemer and sacrificial Lamb made it possible for each of us to enter into the presence of God and to live there.

Entering into any kind of relationship, whether it be as a friend, a parent with a child, in marriage, or with a business partner, brings with it expectations, hopes, and preconceived ideas. However, it is in the reality of the day-to-day circumstances of actually living life together and working together that we learn to know others. That is when we discover what they are really like, if they can be relied upon, if their word has value, whether or not loyalty is part of their being. It is no different with God.

My walk with God began when I was a very small child. I had no thought or concept of being brought to the place where I would sit at His feet, getting to know Him as He revealed Himself to me, being taught by Him, experiencing daily life with Him at the helm.

Personal experience is a valuable instructor, and God is the Master, designing experiences for each of us as individuals. The greatest of teaching tools, those experiences cannot be taken from me. Nor can they be negated. They are mine and mine alone.

Learning at the hand of God, I was taught not only how to live life but how to live it well by living it with Him.

In my late sixties, I began writing, the result of being propelled by the need and desire to tell others of God, His love, and His involvement in everyday life. He sent me to the world with that message—for those who believe and those who do not, for those who are open and those who are closed, for those who are in a church and those who are not, for many and for one.

In this compilation of essays and musings taken from a blog written over a period of four years, I share with you some of those personal experiences from my life. My desire is that you will be pointed to Him and Him alone. May you be provoked to think and to consider things in a new and different light. May you be encouraged, knowing there is a point and purpose to all things. And may you know you are loved and cared for, that you are not alone in this journey called life.

"Here am I. Send me," I answered. And send me He has.

That you might know Me, the one and only true, living God.

Chapter 1

Family

On Family First and the Test of Time

family: n. A group of people who are closely related (by blood, marriage, or adoption); kin.

To stand the test of time: v. To remain useful or valued over a long period of time; to last a long time.

"I'm going to need some help next week." My daughter's statement was followed by a listing of the hours she was scheduled to work and the question, "Is that going to work for you?" For almost ten years, my reply has been, "Yes, it works. It always works." And the coordination of two work schedules, my daughter's and mine, still does.

Being a go-to childcare grandmother has been a priority since the almost ten-year-old was born. Actually, being available for all my grandgirls has always been my first concern since I was given my grandmother's hat. In essence, it has meant being responsive to my three daughters' needs, not just in word but in deed as well.

"Family is what is important." That is the credo of a lifelong friend of mine. Her own childhood family did not exercise that belief. As an adult, it was put into play in her life, and, resoundingly, it has passed the test of time. You'll not find a family anywhere as loyal yet honest with one another and as supportive or willing to work together and fight for one another. They truly are a unit—a family. I have adopted that philosophy as well with that goal in mind for my family.

What does "the test of time" mean? Anything that holds up over time: It may be a friendship or relationship, a personal creed, a lifestyle principle or philosophy, or a way of living. Not needing to be propped up, nurtured, or constantly tended, it is something that stands on its own without support or attention. Not only does it stand, but it also becomes stronger and more solid as time goes on.

Priceless friendships and relationships have passed this test. They are quite simply the ones we can freely and readily return to regardless of the time that has passed or personal input. These stand in sharp contrast to the high-maintenance ones, including those tainted with toxicity and marked by brevity.

Change from the hand of God is another example of those things that pass the test of time. Perhaps we had a personal experience, an epiphany moment, or just an honest look in the mirror, and then we made a decision to live differently—in faith and not for self. The result may be to live without judgment of others, to view life with a positive outlook rather than cynicism, to embrace new and different circumstances in life rather than resisting them, and to be truthful and kind in relationships. Becoming a natural part of us, those changes are foundational, the basis of how we live our lives. And coming from God, they remain untouched and unscathed by time.

In answering my daughter's request for help, I tell her our working relationship has passed the test of time, and it has. In my gardening business, my clientele know the importance of my family. They always respond positively when I need to flex or change my schedule to meet the needs of my children and grandchildren. In these past ten years, there has never been a time when either my family or my clients have been left without much-needed help.

At this point in time in our culture and our society, the family unit has suffered, and its cohesiveness has taken a great toll. Its importance can never be underestimated. Nor should it be ignored. Family as a priority has passed the test of time and is a valuable, fundamental concept with great reward. It has my personal recommendation.

On Mom's Isms

ism: n. An expression or play on words unique to any one person or individual (personal definition).

My mother was a woman of few words. She offered no lengthy monologues expressing her feelings or thoughts but brief, to-the-point statements, what I call isms. These concise sayings were apropos for each occasion or circumstance. It is impossible to mentally retrieve them on command, but during my daily life I often find myself saying, "As my mother would say," and then one of her quotes comes forth.

Here is a collection of Mom's isms from another era and place. For me, they are personal expressions I associate exclusively with her. Perhaps some of them will resonate with you as well, and perhaps they will initiate memories of those in your own life from generations past. Enjoy.

1. "Things could be worse." This was a classic of my mother. It was my chore to dry the dishes she washed by hand. I remember standing at the sink, baring my soul with all the angst of a teenager, and this was her response. Though I never spoke it, I usually thought, *They could be better too.*
2. "Six of one, a half dozen of another." When comparing two things that were similar, this was the ready conclusion. It is one way of saying it really doesn't make any difference and not to belabor the point.
3. "Don't cry over spilled milk." What has happened cannot be changed. There is no going back, no option to do it over again, so just deal with it and don't make a fuss about it.
4. "To each his own." This was my mother's way of expressing the individuality and uniqueness of each person and was her personal acknowledgment that life is lived according to

oneself and no other. Do not judge, and do not waste time trying to figure other people out.

5. "If it was a bear, it would have bitten you." Try explaining this to an eight-year-old who takes everything literally. This is applicable when you've searched high and low for a misplaced item and you find it in an obvious place right under your nose.
6. "You make a better door than you do a window." When the view was blocked, this was Mom's expression—as straightforward and direct as she was.
7. "It'll keep" or "It's not going anywhere." When work was left unfinished or projects were left undone because of other demands of daily life, she had this commonsense approach. There *is* always another day to deal with them.
8. "Don't count your chickens before they hatch." Always practical, Mom kept life grounded on a sane level. Things may not turn out the way you would like. It is better to just wait and see.
9. "I wouldn't lose any sleep over it." Whatever is happening, it isn't worth worrying about.
10. "When it rains, it pours." We have all experienced this one. We just get through a difficult set of circumstances, and another appears. We finally make it through that one, and another rears its ugly head. Generally applied to demanding situations, this refers to the ordeals that can buckle the knees.
11. "Things always come in threes." According to Mom, events came in sets of three. This included both large and small calamities, such as deaths, births, broken dishes, and sicknesses. She had a pretty broad range as to what this covered.
12. "It won't kill you." There was no arguing when she pulled this one out of her arsenal. It didn't matter what my brothers or I didn't want to do or didn't like doing. This one sealed the deal for her. She was right. It wouldn't and didn't kill us.
13. "Were you born in a barn?" I was raised on a farm. This was Mom's admonition when a door was left open.

14. "If I give you an inch, you'll take a mile." I was a difficult child. There was no malice, but I did push the boundaries. My persistence, strong will, and stubbornness caused my parents grief.
15. "Just sleep on it." Mom's sage advice for dealing with problems was passed down from my grandmother. Mom maintained that a solution to a problem or troubling situation would usually come forth in the morning.
16. "Too much of a good thing." *Overstimulation* or *overkill* in today's vernacular happens when fun is no longer fun or excess abounds.
17. "Your eyes are bigger than your stomach." This was an oft repeated saying at family gatherings when there was an abundance of delicious food and people loaded their plates, unable to eat it all.
18. "You bit off more than you can chew." A succinct expression of good intentions with less than ideal results, this was Mom's way of expressing overconfidence.
19. "You're making a mountain out of a molehill" was my mother's practical approach to worrying, overthinking, or creating a problem where one did not exist.
20. "Just between you and me and the fencepost" prefaced an utterance of confidentiality with the unspoken request it not be shared with others.
21. "You can't win for losing." Mom expressed this when criticism and judgment came. It covered those times when, no matter what was done, it wasn't good enough or did not meet someone else's requirements or standards.

"As my mother would say," coming from my own mouth is a gentle reminder of the woman who was in my life for more than forty years. A part of my everyday practical living, her isms will continue to surface for the rest of my life. And perhaps this reinforces the principle as well that what we say matters and lives on long after we are gone.

On Dad, Hoedowns, and Music

music: n. A sound, or the study of such sounds, organized in time; any pleasing or interesting sounds.

hoedown: n. A type of American folk or square dance; the type of music typically played for such a dance.

Love is called the universal language. It is a language spoken and understood by the world's population. My sentiment is that music is on a similar plane. I daresay each culture throughout our world has its own unique form and its own type of music and instruments. It may be the bagpipes of Scotland, the sitar of India, the alphorn of Switzerland, or the dulcimer of Appalachia, but one can hear music and know from what part of the world it originated. It is that singularly identifying.

As part of our unique creation as human beings, music flows from within the heart and the soul. One has only to watch a small child respond to a song, as his or her body begins to sway naturally to the melody and the rhythm. An instinctive reaction when trying to calm an infant or child who is upset, restless, or not feeling well, people hum a soft, gentle tune, which is soothing both to the child and the caregiver.

Try to imagine, if you can, life in our world without music. The silence would be deafening.

Songs serve as memory landmarks in our lives, connecting to events from the past. Often a certain date, place, or circumstance corresponds to the music at that point in time. Words, melodies, and rhythms permeate our beings without our even realizing it. Often we turn to music, or it comes from within us when we are happy, sad, excited, or mad. Even in the deepest, darkest times of life, it is not unusual to seek solace from music.

My father loved music, although I cannot say he loved all music.

He had his definite preferences, and they included marching bands playing John Philip Sousa, male quartets singing hymns, and music from his Texas childhood, what he called hoedown music. Classical music, described as highbrow, and any music with too intense a rhythm were not to his liking.

He was a self-taught musician with the ability to create music from a variety of stringed instruments—banjo, mandolin, fiddle. I grew up with the knowledge that while a fiddle and a violin look alike, there was a vast difference between the two, and that difference lay in the one who played the music. Dad played the fiddle and left the violin to those he deemed sophisticates. The banjo, however, was his first love, and children and grandchildren alike still associate that instrument with him.

Saturday night music fests fill my memories of childhood. Several of Dad's church friends and coworkers from the plywood mill would gather at one of their homes, bringing their instruments and their families with them. Music filled the house for hours on end—music from the Southern part of our country, old gospel songs, and singing galore. I doubt that, like my father, any of those men had a single day of lessons or professional training, but their repertoire of music seemed virtually endless.

Dad never learned to read music, so it was his goal that each of his children would learn to play a musical instrument and have that accomplishment and ability. My two brothers played the baritone, trombone, and accordion. I played the piano. The irony of this is that none of us were taught the instruments and the songs of my father, and a large part of our family heritage is lost, passing away when he did.

My thoughts have been on Dad a lot this past week. I am going to be playing the John Philip Sousa march "Stars and Stripes Forever" as part of the Fourth of July weekend. I am one of the parts, two of the hands in a two-piano, eight-hand performance. Dad would have sat in the audience, his body squared, sitting tall with a huge smile on his face, reveling in it—not only because I was playing—but because there is, after all, nothing like a good Sousa march.

It has always been my thought that I received the gift of music from my earthly father, that it was a genetic trait passed down, a part of my DNA. However, in viewing the common, shared element of music among all people, my conclusion is that the gift was given not only to me but to each of us by our Creator.

While the power of love should never be downplayed, neither should the impact and value of music. Coursing through the veins of all creation, its songs fill the inhabitants of the earth with marvel and wonder. It might be the first warble of a bird at daybreak, the trickling water of a stream traveling over a creek bed, or whales singing their song; or it might be an aria sung by a trained vocalist, the strum of a guitar by a campfire, a small child singing a little ditty as he or she plays, or an outdoor concert in a large amphitheater.

It matters not where one goes or what one does—music will be there. What a gift we have all been given.

> Music speaks what cannot be expressed, soothes the
> mind and gives it rest; heals the heart and makes
> it whole, flows from heaven to the soul.
> —Author unknown

> Then shall all the trees of the forest sing for joy.
> —Psalm 96:12

> Let the floods clap their hands; let the hills sing together for joy.
> —Psalm 98:8

On a Family Bash

A Shanks family reunion has been planned for today. Actually, I refuse to call it a reunion but rather a family bash. After all, who wouldn't prefer going to a bash instead of a reunion? A local swimming pool has been reserved for the afternoon exclusively for the offspring of my own family and those of my two brothers. My thinking is: *If the children have a good time, everyone will.* That's a basic formula for success in a family with kids.

A single thought began rolling around in my mind almost a year ago. I approached family members at Christmas with the possibility of getting together during the summer. Funerals had become the only time of connection, and I wanted that to change.

Childhood memories continuing on into adulthood are filled with family gatherings at the country homes of my grandparents, my parents, or an aunt and uncle. Birthdays were celebrated with a get-together. Holidays meant the house was filled with people—grandparents, aunts, uncles, cousins, nieces, nephews. Summertime included outdoor fun complete with homemade ice cream, the product from my father's herd of milk cows. There was always an abundance of food—hearty, homegrown, and homemade fare prepared by women who knew how to cook.

That changed when my mother's life was taken over by Alzheimer's, and she subsequently passed after a ten-year-long battle. I don't think we ever intended to scatter, but we did. She was the glue that held us together.

Yesterday I tried recalling the last time we were all together. My children and their cousins grew up together, but it has been a long while.

The response to my grand plan has been overwhelmingly positive. I think the lure of the swimming pool worked. The grandgirls are excited over the prospect of getting acquainted with an extended family they've not met before. One grandgirl suggested, "We'll pray before we eat because that's what you do at reunions," and that will be heeded as well. Another grandgirl noted the comment she always hears at reunions is how much she has grown. I need to remember to withhold that remark upon seeing the children of other family members.

Today is also a brother's birthday. It seems fitting we are having a get-together (or rather a bash), even though the homemade ice cream will be absent. An ice cream cake will fill the bill and run a close second as a favorite.

My son is preparing huge slabs of meat for pulled pork sandwiches, and I have no doubt the daughters and granddaughters of the family are continuing the tradition of preparing delectable potluck dishes. The weather is cooperating, and family members have made this day a priority. Can it get any better than this?

A friend asked if I was the family matriarch. "No," I responded. "I just organized it. Besides, don't you have to be old to be one of those?" The answer was that one needs only to be sixty-nine. Bingo!

I'm not certain what it means to be a matriarch, and I'm not taking on that role. However, I *am* thrilled my family is going to be together—and it isn't at a funeral! We will have fun times and good food. What wonderful memories in the making!

On the Things I Have Learned from My Daughters

An older woman about my age was choosing food from the bulk-food bins at the grocery store. Dashing in to purchase my own selection of goodies to fortify me during my workday, I noticed her as I passed by. My one and only thought, a random one coming out of nowhere as it floated through my mind, was, *She must not have daughters.*

My reasoning for this conclusion was that she was wearing a denim jacket with denim jeans. I am no *fashionista*, and, personally, I see nothing wrong with that. However, I have been trained and trained well. If I was to even consider such a combination, there would be a resounding admonition in my head, a collective chorus of voices that would say, "Mom, you can't wear denim with denim!" Who knew? I thought it was enough that they matched.

I have been gifted with three daughters. Actually four, when I include the one who came into my life when my son married, but this is about those who entered my life at birth and grew up under my roof. These girls are not three peas in a pod. If you were to see them in a lineup, you would be hard-pressed to recognize them as siblings. In addition, their personalities and interests differ as much as their physical appearance. They are unique individuals, albeit all raised by the same mother.

That early morning encounter set my mind in gear, and I found myself thinking about those three daughters and all I have learned from them. I know it is the role of the parent to do the teaching, but, oh, the things my girls have taught me.

My daughters have taught me that when decorating a home or planting a garden, one must display pictures or plants in odd numbers, never even. I've learned that accessories—including shoes—and fit make all the difference in creating an outfit of clothing. I have also learned it is not polite to stare at people, and I was recently reminded of that once again.

With three daughters in the house on a school morning, I learned one hot water heater really isn't enough. Their priorities in life are hair and clothing, but loud music, friends, and laughter are of equal importance. Oh, yes, then there are *the boys*. Another lesson I learned was that almost any situation—and the possibilities are far too many to list—has the potential to escalate from minor to major in a heartbeat, and every effort must be taken to avoid that at all cost. Reasoning with a girl who is in a calamitous frame of thinking is nigh unto impossible. Plus, she will either make a lot of noise or go silent. Neither of those two is beneficial or productive.

Each of my daughters taught me no pain or heartbreak could match that of breaking up with a boyfriend. And a mother's love cannot help or heal. Recovery is a solitary, individual process that takes time as well as personal inner strength and resolve. Each daughter made it through those breakups and became stronger young women, and I learned they had to do it on their own.

I am a grandmother now, and I watch as those daughters of mine mother their own daughters. I'm quite certain they are being taught by them as well. All my girls have an open, honest level of communication with their children. It is one I wish I had with them as they were growing up, but I didn't. My grandgirls are encouraged to discuss any and all topics, and they do. What a gift they are being given.

As my daughters have become women, I have learned they never cease being daughters, and I will always be their mother. And yet I have learned a bonus at this time of life, one I never expected in those early days, and it is that of being friends.

I have always maintained that children are gifts, and my daughters are truly that. I have been gifted with a son as well, but I will write about him another day. Besides, he never taught me that wearing denim with denim was inappropriate.

On the Things I Have Learned from My Son

My children are not mine; they are not a possession. They have been given to me to love and to nurture, but ultimately, they do not belong to me. This I learned from the beginning of motherhood when my son, my first child, was born six weeks prematurely. While in early labor at the hospital, a nurse informed me, "This baby cannot be born. It is too little." In my heart I knew otherwise, and the challenge was on as he entered this world within three hours of that statement.

He was small, weighing only five pounds, five ounces, born at a time when the sole treatment for premature infants was to place them in incubators and pump in oxygen. Unable to touch or hold him, I stood there, watching through the glass window of the nursery as his heart beat in his chest like hummingbird wings. It never occurred to me his life could be taken at any point in time. However, later I knew the truth of that.

After ten days in an incubator, we brought him home with all kinds of information regarding what we could expect from a preemie. The pamphlets stated that his physical and mental development would be stunted and that he would be playing catch-up for quite some time. The disparity between reality and what *they* said was evident from the beginning. Within three months' time, he was on par with his peers. Apparently, my son didn't read the handouts. I know God didn't.

Several years later, when he was a young teen, I learned how life can turn in a split second when I received a phone call from the school principal. My son had "taken a little tumble" in PE, but they thought he was okay. They had him sitting up, and "everything seemed to be all right." That *little tumble* resulted in torn ligaments in his neck, making it impossible for them to support his head.

While waiting as the surgeon fused the fourth, fifth, and sixth vertebrae together with bone from his hip and wire configured through them in a figure-eight fashion, I learned to wait on my heavenly Father, asking nothing of Him but knowing my son's future life was not in my hands. The fact that he did not belong to me was reinforced.

He spent the summer in a body cast, which was no small feat for a growing fourteen-year-old boy, and drew questioning looks and stares wherever he went. I watched as he deflected them and simply lived his life, and I learned what it meant to not be affected by others.

Another lesson learned was of the kindness of my Creator. After more than forty years, the only reminders of what could have been a debilitating, life-changing injury are two scars—one on his neck and one on his hip. There have been no complications. I never cease being thankful.

My son taught me a collection can consist of anything. As a little guy, he saved animal figures given out by a local gas station. Empty Jell-O boxes depicting Mr. Jell-O in a variety of flavors filled a drawer. The Jell-O boxes are gone, but he still has the animal figurines he accumulated as a child. The collections of old insulators found along railroad tracks, old bottles recovered from abandoned homes and former dumpsites, seashells from the Gulf of Mexico, Hard Rock Café pins from around the world—I have no doubt they are tucked away as well.

Christmastime brings out displays of more than a few Nativity scenes and favorite Christmas ornaments and decorations. Christmas at his home is like walking into a Christmas gift store. His office is filled with University of Oregon football memorabilia, and his yard with all varieties of unique garden accessories, including a plethora of birdhouses. If he has a particular taste for something, he will make a collection out of it. He just can't help himself.

A classic Renaissance man, his interests are broad. He once had a greenhouse filled with orchids and has created exquisite, detailed cross-stitch hangings. His cooking skills surpass any in the family as he prepares not only Thanksgiving dinner for twenty or more but gourmet meals for guests throughout the year. He has taught me that gender does not confine a person to a box of required or expected behavior.

My son lives life at full speed. He has since birth. A sister commented that he never does anything halfway, and she's right. Witness his passion for nature, wildlife, the sea, and the outdoors; his humor and his laugh; his effort to have a positive outlook no matter what the circumstances; his love for his family, music, and God. If you were to see him, you would be struck by his imposing presence. Everything about him is larger than life.

Despite the fact that he is neither my personal stylist nor interior decorator as my daughters are, I am forever thankful to have him as my son. I continue to learn by having him in my life.

On Grandchildren—Mine

"I'm not old enough to be a grandmother!" is a common cry of women as they learn their first grandchild is on its way. Becoming a grandmother can carry with it perceptions of a stooped-shouldered, white-haired, doddering old woman nearing the end of life. While it is true a grandchild marks the beginning of another branch added to the family tree, that gift brings with it far more than a genealogical marker. From personal experience, being a grandmother is one of the great joys and pleasures in life.

Motherhood began when I was eighteen years old. I was a young mother. Life as a grandmother did not begin until I was fifty-four, but it was well worth the wait. Five grandgirls are now a part of my life, and they are each a treasure.

My oldest grandgirl, the one who made me "Nana," was six months old when I moved in with her, my daughter, and my son-in-law. I lived with them until she was two, and the bond that developed then is tangible and real to this day. We were both early risers, so she and I spent hours together during a time of the day when no one else was awake. I introduced her to Dairy Queen chocolate-dipped cones made with pumpkin ice cream—an annual treat available only around Halloween, zucchini squash, a slew of other vegetables, and eggs over easy. She introduced me to the intensity of loving as a grandmother with the bonus of not being responsible for parenting.

With just the two of us for several years, relinquishing the status of Nana's only grandchild was not easy for a little girl. However, she did as she welcomed four cousins into the family. She is an excellent big sister/cousin, and they adore her. Now a stunning fifteen-year-old with beautiful eyes the size of saucers, a sweet giggle, and a flashing smile, she has introduced me to hip-hop dancing and friendships that exist via texting. And, yes, she still enjoys her vegetables.

Two of my grandgirls (eleven and seven) are moving to the other side of the world. An exaggeration, perhaps, but compared to the short road trip it has taken me to land at their front door since their births, Boise, Idaho, feels a world away.

The older grandgirl in this family, the one I call "the sparkly one," has the most infectious laugh you will ever hear. She devours books, and, with a killer serve and amazing setting skills, she loves volleyball. Add her love of unicorns and sloths to this description, and you can see how broad her interests are.

Her younger sister, "the fearless one," marches to the beat of her own drum. She knows no fear, will try just about anything once (with the exception of food), and has a level of trust that strikes the very depth of panic in a parent or grandparent since she knows no stranger. Place her in a group of adults, and she is as comfortable in conversation as she is with her peers. I am known as "Grandma" to these two.

The other two grandgirls were my next-door neighbors from the time they were born until they moved out of the neighborhood a year and a half ago. That connection earned me the early distinction of "Neighbor Grandma." Since the move, I am now "Gram Gram" or just plain "Gram."

The elder of these, now nine, is an "old soul." She was given that description in infancy, as her eyes could bore a hole through a person, causing one to wonder what she was thinking and seeing. She will never dominate a conversation; she is quiet, but mighty. Her hugs are gentle, with a soft pat on the back, but filled with love. Having saved her from more than a few spiders, I am her heroine.

Her sister, who is seven, was born with a zest for life and a smile on her face. This one knows how to laugh at herself and does so quite frequently. What a gift! I call her my "little pit bull" because she is tenacious, persistent, and spunky. She never willingly concedes a position. With a love for talking, I've often told her that her ears and mouth don't work at the same time, but getting her to listen is generally a futile effort.

While each of my grandgirls is unique, they share the attributes of being strong-willed, stubborn, independent, honest, and outspoken. These are positive, not negative traits, but they can be difficult for parents to deal with. Patience and wisdom are required, and I can appreciate that I am their grandmother not their mother or father.

It is my feeling that the term *blessed* is often overused, misused, and abused. Therefore, it is not one I readily apply. However, in the context and scope of having been given these five gifts from God, I *am* blessed. This grandmother loves her grandgirls—all five of them. Whether I am called Nana, Grandma, Gram Gram, or Gram, from the youngest to the eldest they are my gifts, my treasures, my blessings.

On Hashtags and the Generation Gap

generation gap: n. Differences of opinions, tastes, beliefs, and other social and cultural norms that exist between older and younger age groups, often widened by technological advances.

You know it is going to be a good day when it begins with a gut chuckle and an experience that places a permanent grin on your face. Thus began my day while transporting my grandgirls to school. Mom and Dad were unavailable to shuttle the girls, so I made the forty-five-minute drive from my home to serve as their chauffeur.

The commute to school is unpredictable at best with two grandgirls crammed in the cab of my small pickup with me. One never knows what the dynamics are going to be between the siblings, and the space is crowded and cramped. If they become adversarial, whether verbally or physically, trying to keep the peace while driving can become difficult.

This trip was uneventful until they decided to engage in a hashtag conversation. Twitter is a form of electronic communication, and a tweet is a short message broadcast to the world via that medium. Each electronic comment is prefaced by the symbol for the word hashtag (#), but it was brought to a verbal level by the two girls. "Hashtag, be quiet." "Hashtag, I don't have to." "Hashtag, I don't care." Imagine traveling several miles in a very small vehicle while this takes place.

I asked them to stop, and, of course, I was met with no success. Finally, I said, "Hashtag, settle down." There was drop-dead silence from both of them. Then I heard embarrassed giggles before the older one said, "Somehow that just doesn't sound right coming out of your mouth, Grandma." The laughter rolled from within me, and the stage was set for my own hashtag comments. We were all laughing as I dropped them off at the school door.

Electronics and social media tools are not my niche, so I am quite uninformed as to what is current in that realm. I rely on the grandgirls to operate the television controls. I only learned about FaceTime recently. I have a stupid phone rather than a smartphone. I have a meager idea of what Twitter is and the correlating hashtag. The girls know that about their grandmother, so the grandgirl's comment was an accurate one.

Change has always taken place from one generation to the next. My own age group lives a completely different way of life from that of our parents. The same can be said of us and the generations that follow.

When people do not share common experiences, there is a danger of a separation occurring rather than a uniting, and that can easily happen between generations within a family. I had my own generation gap experience today, though, and it was a positive one—one that bridged two grandgirls and a grandmother, bringing smiles not only today but for quite some time to come.

Stop! Stay! Come!

My daughter proposed a wonderful idea, a grand plan. She had to work in Las Vegas for a week, and she suggested I fly down with the two grandgirls for the weekend. She had a list of things to do, places to see, and activities that were kid-friendly. The dates were set, the plane reservations made, and the trip was set in motion.

Her girls were thrilled for the most part. The one exception was that the one I call the sparkly girl had a grave fear of airplane travel. Not wanting to be left behind and miss out on the possibility of a fun-filled weekend, though, she mustered up all the courage she had and consented. The prospect of seeing Mom at the end of the flight only added to her resolve.

Dad allowed the girls to pack their own backpacks with the instructions that, since they would be carrying them, they needed to be a weight they could handle. What wasn't factored in on the test run—or walk—was the fact that carrying a backpack while walking around the living room is not the same as carrying it a distance through an airport, especially when you are five years old.

Neither of the two adults in this situation did our own TSA check prior to leaving for the airport. Had either of us done so, we would have discovered the little one had filled hers with books, a video game, and as much of her bedroom as possible. It was doubtful she had packed a change of underwear or clothes, but she made certain she was not going to lack for entertainment.

I have parented four children of my own; however, having the responsibility of my grandchildren on such a trek was completely different. Delivering this precious cargo to their mother weighed heavily on me from the beginning.

I knew I was in trouble as soon as we went through the doors heading into the airport terminal. While not a large group—just two small girls—my hope was that I wasn't in over my head. The older one was a sprinter, striding ahead toward only God knows where and what. The younger one lagged behind, sightseeing along the way as she *doopa-dooped*, taking her sweet time.

Gathering them into a huddle, I explained the importance of staying together. I'm certain they heard me. At least, they seemed to be listening. Life in action is often a whole other story, though, isn't it?

The flying experience of this grandmother and her two grandgirls very quickly reached the point of monosyllabic communication. "Stop! Stay! Come!" The first two directives were spoken rather loudly at the one who was heading out, the latter directed at the one who was trailing behind. When we had once again become a group of three, we continued on.

Not far into the trek, the one lagging behind began bemoaning the heaviness of her backpack. Offering to carry it for her, I realized she had a valid point. The weight of all those books made it quite a load.

This scene played out over and over as we made our way toward the plane. Laughter soon took over. They knew what was coming as our group of three spread out. The sparkly one asked, "Grandma, is 'Stop! Stay! Come!' the only thing you know how to say?" I explained to her that it was the only way I could get their attention, that talking to them was ineffective. She giggled.

I think God must feel the same way about me at times. I know what He wants, but I often sprint out with my own plans, my own way. He tries communicating with me, but that is ineffective when dealing with headstrong determination. Upon running into a wall, I do *stop*. And when there is nowhere for me to go and no other options, I *stay*. Once I realize and reconcile the fact that His way is the better way, He says, "Come!" and the two of us head off once again. As with the grandgirls, the base is love.

Sometimes I find myself wondering how I am going to be remembered when life in this form has come to an end. I have no doubt that for two of my grandgirls, that memory will be condensed into these three words—"Stop! Stay! Come!"

On Hypocrisy

hypocrisy: n. The practice of engaging in the same behavior or activity for which one criticizes another; moral self-contradiction.

"Practice what you preach. Words are cheap. Actions speak louder than words. Do as I say, not as I do." These are all variations on the same theme—hypocrisy.

No lesson is quite as effective as that taught by a child. While helping two of my grandgirls get ready for school one day, I ran headlong into my own personal tutoring session on hypocrisy.

As the girls ate breakfast, the older one dived into a bowl of cereal, a type she hadn't eaten before. She commented she didn't like it. I suggested she try another bite. After several more tastes, her assessment remained the same—she didn't like it. Having been raised by a mother for whom throwing away uneaten food was almost a cardinal sin, I was reluctant to discard it and tried cajoling her into eating it.

The little one put in her two cent's worth: "Why does she have to eat it if she doesn't like it?" Have I mentioned having a verbal exchange with this one is comparable to trying to run a marathon with a pit bull attached to your ankle? I gave it my best effort, but she didn't give up, and she did have a point. If I don't like the taste of a food, I don't eat it. There you go—a muffin with cream cheese for brain food instead of cereal as the two headed off to school.

We have all had our own observations of and/or experiences with blatant hypocrisy—the minister who preaches of purity and righteousness from the pulpit only to have his private, personal life revealed in lurid detail; the politician who espouses representing his constituents with integrity and the ensuing exposure of fraudulent behavior at the expense of the very ones he represents. Then there are those personal one-on-one experiences. On any level, hypocrisy evokes a very real sense of betrayal because it *is* just that—betrayal, reinforced by actions of disloyalty and deception.

I am, however, addressing the more subtle kind of hypocrisy, the kind that masquerades itself as a caring, nurturing parent, grandparent, or friend. How many times do we make a suggestion to another regarding something we never apply to ourselves or are incapable of controlling and mastering within our own lives? For example, it is so easy to tell others how to lose weight, gain health, save money, organize their lives, raise their children, control their anger. I am of the thought that if I am not living it, I do not own it and have no right to speak of it to another.

Since my cereal experience with the grandgirl and the introduction of the concept of *hypocrisy* into my thinking, I have been resisting the idea of making personal application of it. *Me? A hypocrite?* Can you hear the tone of dumbfoundedness in my voice and visualize the expression of incredulity on my face? Surely not! The truth is that in that interaction I was a hypocrite. Trying to get my grandgirl to *do as I say, not as I do* is the very manifestation of hypocrisy.

While mowing lawns today, my personal therapy session in my gardening business, I found myself thinking about these things. I wonder how many times and in how many different ways I am guilty without even realizing it. I am quite certain that wasn't the first time, nor will it be the last.

Thanks to an eight-year-old pit bull of a grandgirl, I was able to see myself through her eyes. She put me on alert, and for that I am thankful. Besides, she'll have no problem calling me out in the future if necessary.

> Out of the mouths of babes.
> —Psalm 8:2

On Turning Ten

The nine-year-old grandgirl is turning ten in three weeks. "Double digits," she points out. This birthday is a landmark one. As a nearly seventy-year-old grandmother with more than a few double-digit birthdays in my experience, I still remember the excitement around that first one.

This grandgirl has been waiting for this special birthday for months. I am quite certain something magical is about to occur. It is akin to being old enough to enter school, get one's driver's license, vote—all those events that require being a certain age. This one is mental, though. I am unable to think of anything that specifies the need to be at least ten years old as a requirement for participation other than amusement parks or swimming pools.

Turning ten carries with it the real sense of growing up. No longer a little kid, middle school will soon be at hand, and the teen years and high school are just around the corner. New rights and privileges are added daily by parents as they witness a different type of maturity and personal responsibility develop within their child. Aware of the fact that she is getting older, this grandgirl is stepping into that role. It is a pleasure to watch, a joy to observe.

Plans for a birthday party are underway, and I have been invited. In fact, she presented me a handmade invitation. While it included the date and location for the pool party, there was a side note that said, "Try to bring a present." I laughed, but its diplomacy does bear out my point. She is growing up, and it is happening right before my eyes.

Happy birthday, sweet girl!

On Fun in a Box

The week before Easter, two of my four children received notice they had lost their jobs. In fact, they were informed of such within three days of one another. The clothing company my daughter worked for declared bankruptcy without warning. The bank where my son had worked more than twenty years consolidated two areas, and he found he was the odd man out. When the family got together on Easter, there was no pall cast upon us, but there was talk of unemployment, its ramifications, and the uncertainty of the future. It is difficult to ignore such a drastic change in the lives of family members. Nor did we want to.

Easter Sunday was a glorious sunny day, one that is not guaranteed at that time of year in the Pacific Northwest. The family gathered outside on the patio, my son-in-law tending the meat on the grill, the cousins running back and forth playing together.

Another of my daughters brought out a small box of jelly beans, something she had purchased while traveling. Labeled *Bean Boozled*, I call it "Fun in a Box" because it was—such fun, that is.

These appeared to be ordinary jelly beans. In reality, they were anything but ordinary. Regular, tasty candies were mixed with those that had vile, disgusting, outrageous flavors. Choosing an appetizing one was a Russian roulette of sorts. Each color was identified on the back of the box as either/or (e.g., mint or vomit), but that determination was unknown until the jelly bean was placed in the mouth.

It was "Game On!" Three of the siblings and a brave eight-year-old granddaughter began taking turns. The expressions on their faces were indescribable as they gingerly put a jelly bean in their mouth, waiting for the moment it made its way to their taste buds and the realization that came thereafter. When the flavor was good, their face lit up as they chewed and swallowed. When the jelly bean fell into the other category, they headed for a garbage can with contorted face and the sound of gagging. Laughter filled the air as this process was repeated over and over again.

The box held flavors that would cause anyone to recoil—skunk, stinky socks, lawn clippings, baby wipes, toothpaste, moldy cheese, rotten egg, and others. Why anyone would continue going back for more, I have no idea, but they did. Those of us observing this scene were highly amused as we all heartily laughed.

The brave grandgirl chose one that was either popcorn or booger. Yes, I said *booger*. Popping it in her mouth, she chewed and tasted. Oh no! It was booger! Her approach was to discard the revolting candy and then head into the kitchen for an aerosol shot of whipped cream before coming back for more, cleansing her palate as it were. A most memorable reaction was when my son chomped down on one that tasted like canned dog food. He has a cast-iron stomach, but I thought he was going to lose it on that one!

In spite of the upheavals in this family's circumstances, we were given a gift of fun and laughter in a little box. This came at a time when we were remembering the death and resurrection of Christ, God's gift to the world, the One who defeated death and made it possible that we might live our lives with God and with joy. Easter 2014 was a good day.

On Firsts and Lasts

It was my last opportunity to watch the eleven-year-old grandgirl play volleyball—perhaps for a long while. This sparkle of a girl with a contagious laugh is moving a distance away. The forty-five-minute drive to her home, which makes possible my involvement in her daily life and events, will be replaced by one that takes several hours.

I remember when she was born. I remember the first time I held her.

Firsts and lasts—so much of life is measured in those two terms. How often do we say, "That was the first time . . ." or "I remember the last time . . ."?

Life began at birth as a blank book, with the ensuing script filling the pages to include an endless variety of firsts. Each of us had a first introduction to life outside the womb and a first interaction with our caregivers. We experienced a first cry, a first smile, a first step, and a first day of school. Perhaps a first kiss, a first job, marriage, and a new home followed, and then even more firsts came when a child joined the family.

Then there are the lasts—the last day of school and graduation for an offspring, the last night he or she spends at home before leaving the nest, the last day at work before retirement, a last good-bye, the last contact with a loved one before his or her passing.

First and lasts—often they are milestones, cairns in life's journey, a mental vehicle to navigate through memories, a method to ground us in the ever-changing experiences and circumstances of life.

The first day of life also brings with it the last day of life. Each of us has individual, personal books with a beginning and an end. It is those chapters, however, that fill the pages, that truly matter—the manner in which life is lived. Nothing is more important than living life well and living it in truth and light.

My personal conviction is that the last day of one's life, the physical, is the first day of another, the eternal. In the next life there is no *last*, as that *is* what eternity is—without end. That reality, that truth, should never be minimized, overlooked, or lost as we live out our physical lives.

Thankfully, as I watched my grandgirl play volleyball, I wasn't of the mind-set it might be a last time. That would have taken away from the pure pleasure and joy I have as I watch her. Actually, I think I can easily plan a trip to Idaho during volleyball season. And that will be a first, but not a last.

On the Thinking Part of Your Mind

The little one and I sat watching as the older sister played her softball game, and we were talking, which is something she does quite a lot of. But then, so do I, so the conversation flows when we're together. I reminded her of a ball field in the area where she had played earlier in the season, but she couldn't remember where it was.

"Think," I said. "Just think."

"First, I have to find the thinking part of my mind," she responded.

Using two of her little girl fingers as pretend legs, she began "walking" them all over her head, searching for that area. She has a nonstop giggle and the ability to talk and giggle at the same time. So she did that while covering her entire head, citing the areas she found—the food part, the dance part, the school part, the play part—but, alas, the thinking part remained elusive.

One need not look far to see this happens quite often with people—the inability to find and use the thinking part of their minds. At least she tried.

On Learning to Be Content

content: adj. Satisfied about a particular circumstance; thus, in a state of satisfaction.

My youngest daughter and her husband are leaving this morning, and they are taking two of my grandgirls with them—the eleven-year-old sparkly grandgirl and the nearly eight-year-old fearless one. The move has been common knowledge for several months, but as often happens, time has flown all too quickly. And here we are.

This mother and grandmother has been spoiled, and I openly, unashamedly, and unabashedly admit it. For the past eight years, I have been most fortunate to be able to be at the doorstep of my daughter and her family with a short road trip. That changes today as this part of the family heads for Idaho.

I have learned to be content, whatever state I'm in. This has been floating through my mind for days. I would be lying through my teeth, however, if I stated contentment has been my mainstay as the countdown to moving day has taken place. In fact, during the past week, the opposite has come to bear.

Yesterday, while on yet another emotional roller coaster filled with sadness and a big lump in the back of my throat, I came to my senses. This move is not separate from the hand of my heavenly Father, and just because it isn't to my liking does not mean it isn't good. "Help me," I requested, and He has.

Once my head was screwed on straight, I was able to think about that scriptural admonition a bit more clearly. In the simplest of terms, it means having a sense of happiness and being satisfied regardless of the situation or circumstances. It goes hand in hand with having peace within rather than all-consuming turmoil. That can only come from the knowledge that my Creator is One who loves and cares not only for me but for my family as well.

Life and the living of it are never static; they are ever-changing.

Opportunity is presented at the hand of God in ordinary daily life to learn, to grow, to become the person we were each created to be. Learning is an ongoing process. Sometimes we revel in that process; other times we abhor it—often because of a lack of understanding. Nonetheless, I am of the belief that there is purpose in all things.

Part of my family moving to Idaho is in His plan. Am I content in that? I can honestly say I am learning to be. In fact, I am only too aware there are several other areas in my life where this pearl of wisdom needs to be applied as well. There is always more work that needs to be done in this life of mine.

I have learned, in whatsoever state I am, therewith to be content.
—Philippians 4:11 (KJV)

On Children, Shining Stars, and Kindness

kindness: n. The state of being kind; instance of charitable behavior.

The little one had left her star in the classroom, and she hurried back to retrieve it. Made of blue construction paper with her name on it, she informed her older sister and me it was her fourth shining star. She had received more shining stars this year than anyone else in her class. My thought was that this second-grader was a teacher's dream of a student, one who followed instructions, sat quietly, and was a good citizen, and she had been rewarded with such a treasure. As we placed it on the refrigerator alongside her other stars, I told her how proud I was of her.

It wasn't until the next day that I learned the story behind *this* very special shining star. Social interaction does not come easily for all children. For some, relating to others is most difficult, so they withdraw, retreating into themselves. These are often the ones on the outer fringes of a group, isolated and alone. The school classroom with all its chaos and activity is troubling and unsettling for them.

The teacher had given free choice to her students, the equivalency of a twenty-minute recess in the classroom. This grandgirl chose to play with a little guy who struggles, one who doesn't come close to being the social butterfly she is. (But, regardless of age, there aren't many who can match her on that plane.) What Mrs. Dickson took note of, however, was that she was the only one who played with him, and the two played together the entire time. Her shining star was a very observant teacher's acknowledgment of that.

Kindness is a quality not spoken of much these days. One hears, "Be nice, be civil, be compassionate, be supportive, be a team player," but very little is said about being kind. An innate trait, there is a natural follow-through, with one's actions and behavior manifesting it.

In our society, much emphasis is placed on the need for adult role models for our children. While this is a valid and important point, we often fail to recognize that children possess the same qualities—or lack thereof—as adults. I would maintain the real role models are our children, who live their lives unencumbered by correctness and games, with openness, honesty, and purity. It would behoove all of us, myself included, to follow the lead of a small child with her shining star and her very kind spirit.

What would our homes and families, our neighborhoods and schools, our workplaces, and our society and world be like if just this one virtue was put into practice?

A little bit of kindness goes a long way.

> Be kind to one another.
> —Ephesians 4:32

On Homecoming and Timing

timing: n. The time when something happens.

Timing is everything. In fact, life is all about the timing. From conception to death, it is the synchronization of details in life that place people in a specific place at a specific time. Having to stop for a red light, an unplanned conversation with a store clerk, a forgotten item that needs to be retrieved before leaving the house, a search for a child's missing shoe—it takes so little for a sequence of events to be altered. People control very little, least of all the timing of anything.

Animal migration is a superb example of the importance of timing. Found in all major animal groups, including birds, mammals, fish, reptiles, amphibians, insects, and crustaceans, migration is a relatively long-distance movement that usually occurs on an annual cycle. It may be triggered by local climate changes, the availability of food, or mating. Driven by a natural instinct, whole species would disappear were it not for the migratory patterns that bring them to food when one food source has disappeared, providing an environment for procreation as well.

The fifteen-year-old grandgirl suggested, "Nana, you should write about it. You talk all the time about perfect timing."

I had lived with the one who made me a grandmother and her family for one-and-a-half years from the time she was six months old. We were roommates, the two of us sharing a very small bedroom. I was present for a long list of firsts—first baby immunizations, first steps, first Christmas morning, first birthday, first trip to Disneyland. She and I were both very early risers, so the early morning hours belonged to us. It would not be stretching the truth to say we had our own "mutual admiration society."

The day had included lunch with several of my high school classmates in a small town north of where I lived. I knew I would have time to get some work done afterward, so I put my work clothes in the truck, planning on stopping by my daughter's house to change. It was then just a short jaunt to the task of cutting back ivy.

This was the middle of the week, so I wasn't expecting to see my grandgirl. I was informed, however, that she was upstairs. "Helloooo," I shouted up the staircase. "Why aren't you in school?" The answer came down that it was a scheduled half-day for school.

"You're here just in time," my daughter said. A young man was on his way to extend an invitation to homecoming, and I had arrived on-site at the exact time he was supposed to show up.

When you see my eldest grandgirl, her eyes are the first thing you notice, and then you see the smile. You get the whole package all at once—a pop, a flash of life. These two teens have been good friends for quite a while, and I have no doubt he has been mesmerized.

She came down the stairs, having received a phone call and the request that she meet him out front. With excited anticipation, she walked out the door.

Having gone to a great deal of time and thought, he had written a message by incorporating a variety of candies secured to a large poster board. I'm quite sure a roll of Lifesavers was one of them, along with the invitation to "Be my Lifesaver and go to homecoming with me."

Impressed by the effort he had put forth, I was also delighted to be part of this event in my grandgirl's life. After he left, my daughter, grandgirl, and I talked about the perfect timing that made it possible for me to be present.

My heavenly Father created the physical universe and all that is in it to function with precision. The Master Choreographer, He has meticulously planned and designed my life with exactness as well. As water flows down a streambed in its natural course, heading for the ocean, I follow as He leads and guides me. I am not the author of my own destiny.

Not a moment too soon, not a moment too late. My heavenly Father gave me a gift today as I shared another first in the life of a precious grandgirl—her first official homecoming invitation. Our experiences are not only part of a greater whole. They are personal gifts as well. And it is all about the timing—His timing.

On Cheek Exercise

laugh: v. To show that you are happy and that you think something is funny by smiling and making a sound from your throat; an experience of mirth peculiar to the human species.

laughter: n. The sound of laughing.

It was the end of a weekend filled with food, family, and fun. Doubled over at the waist, gasping for air while laughing, one of my daughters declared, "I've laughed so hard my cheeks hurt."

"That's a good thing," her sister responded, inflating and deflating her cheeks—vaguely resembling a puffer fish. "You're getting cheek exercise." The laughter began again, sounds of joy and delight filling the evening air.

Family times with sisters and cousins are infrequent since my youngest daughter's family moved out of the area two years ago. The girls' weekend was planned to bring us together—nine females in one house, ranging in age from nine to seventy-one.

In all honesty, I approached this time together with cautious anticipation, my mother/grandmother radar checking for potential conflicts. That is a lot of females gathered in one place for three days and three nights.

The caution was all for naught. The fact that laughter dominated our time together was above and beyond what I could have hoped for.

I love to laugh. There was a long span of time in my life when I did not know laughter, a time when deep, dark depression enveloped me like a stifling blanket of fog. The abysmal darkness and hopelessness surrounded me, and I wasn't sure if I was going to survive.

It is my personal belief that God has the best sense of humor in the world, and, since we are created in His image, it is natural that we would be given a sense of humor as well. And, yes, since He laughs we laugh too.

As those personal times of depression began to lessen, laughter and humor began to flourish in my life. I cannot fathom living life without these treasured gifts given by Him.

We have all heard the phrase "Laughter is the best medicine." Packing a wallop of truth, it isn't just a cute catch phrase. Laughter *is* a powerful antidote to stress, pain, and conflict.

Having the attribute of being infectious, it is far more contagious than a cough, sniffle, or sneeze. When others are laughing, it is difficult to not be drawn in. In fact, laughing with other people is more powerful than laughing alone. Shared, it brings people together in happiness.

Physical as well as emotional benefits are gained from laughter. It is said to trigger healthy physical changes, including strengthening and boosting one's immune system by decreasing stress hormones and increasing immune cells and infection-fighting antibodies, thus improving resistance to disease.

Laughter boosts your energy, diminishes pain, and relaxes one's whole body, the effects remaining for forty-five minutes. Who knew?

When a person engages in laughter, the release of endorphins is triggered. The body's natural feel-good chemicals, they promote an overall sense of well-being. One cannot feel anxious, sad, or angry while laughing. Laughing just makes you feel better.

A potent dose of laughter also helps the heart, improving the function of blood vessels and increasing blood flow, a protection against heart attack and cardiovascular problems.

I laughed and laughed this past weekend. And then I laughed some more, getting a hefty amount of "cheek exercise." The time spent with my three daughters and five grandgirls will forever be a part of me, the memories of the sounds of laughter filling my being and my soul. I could not have asked for more.

May your days and your lives be filled with laughter as well. May you laugh. And then may you laugh some more. Laugh so hard your cheeks hurt, so that you, too, get cheek exercise. It's good for you! Or as my mother would say, "It's good for what ails you."

A cheerful heart is a good medicine.
—Proverbs 17:22

Blessed are you who weep now, for you will laugh.
—Luke 6:21

On People First

sacrifice: n. Selfless, good deeds for others; surrender or giving up anything for the sake of something or someone else.

Supper, not dinner, was the name given to the evening meal in my childhood home, and it was a most basic fare. A dish created out of necessity by my mother-in-law decades ago is known in my family as "Grandma's macaroni and tomatoes." I had purchased the necessary ingredients to prepare it the last time I shopped, although the bell peppers and kidney beans were my embellishments, not hers. Her meal, which was often prepared for children home from school at lunchtime, consisted of crisping bacon, sautéing onions in the grease, and adding macaroni and tomatoes, a filler dish readily made with home-canned tomatoes.

As I began preparing it, chopping the vegetables and frying the bacon slices, my thoughts were on the woman who was a part of my life for more than thirty years.

For her, meal preparation was done on a woodburning cookstove, even after electric ranges were available to the general population. She worked in the kitchen alone, often cooking for an army—hungry adult men and their families, including lots of children. When holidays came, she made certain a favorite pie had been made for each and every person at her table. Pies lined every available counter space, memories in the making. No one helped with meal preparation or cleanup, and she did not own a dishwasher. She was the sole cook and bottle washer.

What stands out about this woman, one who had the most minimal of resources with which to work, is the fact that no one was ever turned away from a meal or from her home. If you were in her home at mealtime, you were fed and fed well—not lavishly, but no one ever had reason to leave the table hungry. If someone needed a place to stay, she made certain room was found.

People come first. This principle for living, this admonition and adage was introduced to me many years ago and has become a part of me, its value and importance reinforced over and over again.

Putting people first and sacrifice go hand in hand. One cannot and does not put others first without that thread of selflessness running through one's being. It is an unconscious characteristic, the natural state of a person, one where no ulterior motives are involved, no thought of debt being owed or of recompense.

You simply place another's needs or desires ahead of your own. It is giving time when someone asks. It is giving an ear to hear, to listen. It is being available, giving of yourself. In its literal sense, it is putting others ahead of yourself.

Another aspect of this charge is that people are more important than any material thing. I could have virtually every object money could buy, but without people in my life, I would be a shell of a person. People are more important than power, prestige, social status, or financial gain. People are eternal. That application cannot be made to an antique, an expensive piece of jewelry or clothing, or the best automobile or home money can buy.

There is no age differentiation in the directive to put people first. It doesn't matter whether a person is young, a teen, middle-aged, or elderly. So when a little munchkin accidentally breaks a priceless treasure, remember that the child is important, not the object. When a drink is spilled inside a vehicle, which has the soul—the car or the one who did the spilling? When an important conversation is taking place, allow time for the one who needs to vent, to voice, to be heard.

This principle is not limited to or defined by only those who are family and friends. The world is filled with people who simply need someone to notice and care.

How one lives is important to consider. Life can be lived well . . . or not so well. My observations and firsthand experience cause me to recommend this foundational building block of life as a worthy goal.

Grandma's hospitality and sacrifice are a prime example of putting people first in a practical way. I am an advocate for personal change and growth at the hand of my Creator. This principle is one to be prized, its worth never underestimated.

Just imagine a world where this philosophy is a way of life. It will only happen at the hand of God.

Chapter 2

Gifts, Treasures, and Blessings

On Gifts from the Past

Mom's rose is clearly visible from my kitchen window. I planted it where it can be seen daily, regardless of the season. The rose and I lived in temporary circumstances for quite a while before we were each given a place to call home, a place to put down our roots and become established. The rosebush had spent several years in a large container, given foster care by my daughter while I passed through several apartments and interim housing on my pathway to permanency.

As a surprise gift, Dad gave me the rosebush after Mom passed away. This start from her favorite rose was just a tiny thing, rooted from a stem he cut and placed in the ground. Dad was a farmer, not a gardener. That he took the time and made the effort to propagate a rose cutting with me in mind makes it that much more meaningful.

Given the length of time civilization has been in existence on this earth, the advent of nurseries and garden centers—where plants, shrubs, and trees are readily available for purchase—has been a recent development.

Prior to that, plant sharing and seed exchanges between neighbors and friends formed the foundation of gardens. Often a cutting—usually a stem, leaf, or root from a plant—was placed either in water or moist soil to promote growth. Perhaps a shrub was rooted by simple layering—bending and burying a low-growing branch in the ground. Or the roots of perennial flowers were separated, divided, and shared. Scions, branches cut from fruit trees, were either placed in a planting medium where they took root or grafted onto other fruit trees—the beginnings of new orchards or expansion of existing ones. Vegetable and flower plants were allowed to fully mature, and the seedpods removed, saved, and exchanged. For centuries, these were the methods used for proliferation of house plants, vegetable and flower gardens, and orchards.

What is it about gifted plants—either starts, seeds, or plants that come from another method—that makes them special? Over the years my own garden has been filled with them: daffodil bulbs given by an aunt, a mother, a grandmother; an intoxicatingly fragrant *Daphne odora,* the cutting taken one Sunday morning after church by my mother from one at my childhood church home and placed in a little container of water on the kitchen windowsill to root; a Joseph's Coat Climbing Rose transplanted from my daughter's garden; raspberry starts from my father's patch; a peony root given by an elderly client just before she passed away; and a hearty fuchsia shrub from my mother-in-law, its origins going back to her ancestral home. There are plenty of plantings in my garden gifted by a friend whose own garden had to be deer-proof. However, when the deer ignored the deer-resistant plant list, I received several of her shrubs.

Nurseries are filled with plants, shrubs, and trees to buy, but none carry the emotional significance of those that have been given, shared, and/or passed down. Gardens are a living thing, always a work in progress. On a personal level, gifted plants carry with them a sense of the one who gave them. When I tend those plants and shrubs shared by friends and family, I am reminded of them, their presence, and their roles in my life. As I look out the window at my beautiful rose with its stunning blooms, I do not see just a plant. I see Mom's rose, and I remember those who bore me, raised me, loved me, and who are no longer on this earth. It is a treasured gift, in plain view from my kitchen window.

This past fall, I took several cuttings from that same rosebush, placed them in soil, and covered them with plastic containers. At Christmastime, after checking for roots, they were lovingly transplanted into containers prepared with beautiful composted soil and given to each of my four children. In this first summer of life, there are reports of blooms. Mom's rose has been perpetuated to bring pleasure to her grandchildren. These living gifts from the past carry forward into the future.

On the Gift of Sight

Not all that long ago contact lenses and LASIK surgery were not commonplace, and glasses were patently prescribed for vision correction. A common adage from that era, "I don't need glasses except to see," is a perfect description of the condition of my eyesight. Distance vision is decent, not perfect, but somewhere between my youth and the present I developed the need for some serious corrective lenses in order to read or do any handwork. In the face of that reality, I have resorted to using reading glasses. The only problem is finding them when I need them since I have a habit of pulling them off without thought and randomly setting them down after using them.

Many years ago I had a dream. In that dream I was declared legally blind. In the physical realm, legal blindness is a severe visual impairment or loss of vision. Whereas good vision is described as 20/20, which means one is able to read an eye chart clearly at a distance of twenty feet, legal blindness is ascribed at 20/200 or worse. To better understand this, a person with minimal vision is able to see at twenty feet what one with good vision can see at two hundred feet.

There are two ways of viewing anything—from a physical perspective, that which is seen with the physical eyes, or from a spiritual perspective, that which is seen only with spiritual eyes. Upon awakening from that dream, I knew I had been shown a picture of the state of my spiritual vision.

One might ask, "Why is spiritual sight important? How is one able to see that which is unseen? Why does it matter in *my* life?"

In my experience, when life—and that word covers a very broad spectrum—is seen only through one's physical eyes, the picture is restricted. It's like viewing the underside of the proverbial tapestry rather than seeing it from the top. It's the same as when I try to read without my reading glasses. I know something is on the page, but I am unable to discern what is there.

We live in a spiritual world. What is seen with the physical eye is not the real world but a front, a façade. A whole level of spiritual activity goes on beyond what we see and experience with our natural eyes and senses. The spiritual realm is actually ground zero, the base for all that takes place in our lives, our planet, and the universe. The importance of being aware of that and having spiritual sight can never be underestimated because it is where life really happens. Things are not as they seem to be.

It is my belief that humans are created in the image of God—a spiritual entity, not just a physical one. Therefore, it is not unreasonable that spiritual vision goes hand in hand when living life with Him. Seeing that which is unseen takes place within a person's self. The spirit of God connects with the spirit of humankind, resonating within one's soul. Perhaps it is, indeed, an epiphany experience, a moment of illumination or discovery. Perhaps it's a single thought, an awareness or sense, a visual picture that comes into one's mind, or a dream. Knowledge given from God means knowing something we didn't know we knew. "I see," said the blind man. That itself is an apt characterization.

Perception, a gift given by God, can never be achieved through self-effort. A night-and-day difference exists in everyday life between viewing just the outer, which is one-dimensional, and seeing beyond appearances and superficiality into the inner.

To have spiritual vision is to see as God sees, where undeniable truth prevails. It is seeing what is, not what appears to be, and it is the only way one can see and know what is true and absolute. The natural result of walking with Him and living life with Him, it is what happens when one rubs shoulders with excellence. The alternative is that of functioning in darkness as one who is blind.

In my frustration over having only a single pair of reading glasses, I have purchased several and positioned them throughout the house, in my purse, and in the truck. On a good day, I should be able to find at least one pair. The added bonus is I don't need *any* glasses to have 20/20 spiritual vision.

> We look not on what can be seen, but at what cannot be seen; for what can be seen is temporary, but what cannot be seen is eternal.
> —2 Corinthians 4:18

On the Gift of Water

Simple columns of basalt of varying form and height, some six feet or more tall, stood on display at a business that sold stone for landscaping. Classic beauty, stoic in stature, each had a hole bored up through the center so it could be used as a fountain for a water feature. Visible from the busy highway, these rock features caught my eye the first time I saw them as I drove past.

My needs are basic, my wants few, so when I found myself yearning for a plain columnar rock, it seemed unusual. Each time I passed by, the desire for a basic rock form was reinforced—a desire with no hope of being fulfilled. As an apartment dweller, any prospects of ever having a pond with a pillared rock as the fountain were pretty far-fetched. Besides, I was quite certain the price tag of ownership was far beyond anything I could ever afford. So I admired them longingly from afar.

Doors opened, and I had the opportunity to have my own house. Along with it came a gift of money—a housewarming gift. While picking up some rock for a client at that same business, I decided to check the prices of the rock columns. What a pleasant surprise when I realized the size I would need, about two-and-one-half-feet tall, was within my price range! Decision made—one columnar rock purchased, one pond in the works.

There are pros and cons to being a single person. Delegation is not an option for me. However, I have done things I never conceived of doing, and there is a sense of accomplishment that comes with that. Creating a pond falls in that category.

I knew I wanted the pond outside my kitchen window, where I could hear it from inside. I started digging and digging . . . and digging some more, until I connected with an underground drain pipe, which determined the depth. I spent hour upon hour shaping that empty hole, laying out the liner, and getting the pump in place, then bringing in the rock and plantings needed to naturalize it. A man could probably have accomplished the same job in one-tenth the time, but this was my project, my pond.

My son-in-law manhandled the rock column into place for me, but I did the plumbing. Hands-on experience is a valuable instructor, and the first time I turned the water on, I realized the fittings needed to be glued. Mistakes were made, but lessons were also learned. I then glued the PVC pipe together using the purple primer and cement that plumbers use. And used correctly, it does hold.

Observing the water come up and out of that basalt column reminded me of an Old Testament story. The children of Israel had been living in bondage in Egypt for more than four hundred years and were promised freedom by God. After many confrontations between Moses and Pharaoh during which God brought down numerous plagues on that land, they were led away under the guidance of Moses, God's chosen leader. Wandering in the desert as they ventured forth to the Promised Land, they had no water to drink, a formidable situation for such a large population. God instructed Moses to strike a rock with his staff. When he did, water gushed forth abundantly, and the people and their livestock drank. In my mind's eye, it came from the center of that rock just as mine does.

In the physical world, water is one of the most important substances on earth. Two-thirds of the earth's surface is covered by water. The human body consists of 75 percent water. A human can go for more than three weeks without food, but the maximum time an individual can go without water has been estimated at a week, though that is generous. Three to four days is more typical. Clearly, water is one of the prime elements responsible for life on this earth.

Spiritually speaking, water is even more important than in the physical realm since it represents life, which is eternal. "The river of the water of life, bright as crystal, flowing from the throne of God" (Revelation 22:1).

I believe when a heart's desire is granted, especially one that carried with it an impossibility and improbability of ever being realized, there is a greater appreciation for its attainment in comparison to things that are easily obtained. In my experience, the longing and waiting for what seems impossible enhances the fulfillment, making it a cherished gift.

My pond fits that description. It is a thing of beauty and brings me a great deal of pleasure. Whether I'm in my backyard or listening through my open kitchen window, its gurgling and splashing sounds soothe and bring peace as well as a sense of stillness—the renowned water effect. I love the good feelings that come from being around water.

With its pillared fountain and the accompanying music to my ears, this water feature never loses its appeal. It's a gift for which I am always grateful. Even more so, I am eternally grateful for the gift of living water so freely given by God, the Creator of all.

> Everyone who drinks of this water will be thirsty again,
> but those who drink of the water that I will give them will
> never be thirsty. The water that I will give will become
> in them a spring of water gushing up to eternal life.
> —John 4:13–14

On a Gift from the Heart

When the package was delivered to me, I found a handmade quilt neatly folded and tucked inside a fabric case of plain blue chambray. Pinned closed with a safety pin along the open edge, a small plastic bag secured to the case held a picture of several women displaying the gift along with a letter and a small booklet, a Gospel of John.

Written to the recipient and signed by the ones who made it, the letter read:

> Dear Quilt of Honor Recipient,
>
> The Threadbearers are a group of quilters that meet at Harbor Baptist Church in Winchester Bay, Oregon. We want to thank you for your service to our country. May this quilt bring comfort and love. Your service is appreciated. May God richly bless you.

More than just a quilt constructed from fabric of a patriotic theme, it was a gift from the heart. The craftsmanship was outstanding, a beautiful piece of work. The love and the sincerity with which the quilt was made and given was palpable, powerful, and real.

It was my privilege to deliver this gift to a veteran, a longtime friend since grade school, honoring and acknowledging his service to his country fifty years ago. The bonus was that it was a surprise, an unexpected delivery.

The Threadbearers originated in 2003 with one woman who had a vision and a desire. Now a group of ten to fifteen quilters, most of them retirees, they can be found on any given Monday morning in a church basement, designing and creating quilts to be given to the men and women in their local community who have served in the US military. Many of these quilters feel it is their personal ministry, a way of expressing God's love and saying thank you to some who may have been forgotten. Each quilt is unique, as the intent is to make them as individual as each recipient.

These women are the quiet ones among us, the humble, the ones who have no desire to draw attention or to make names for themselves. They do not seek recognition but are fulfilling a mission, one they feel passionate about.

The recipients are often the quiet ones as well, at least when speaking about themselves and their service in the military. Reticent and often reluctant to share, many of them carry a heavy burden, unseen by acquaintances, friends, and family.

War is heinous, its atrocities horrific. Having served in Vietnam, the Persian Gulf, Iraq, Afghanistan, or other places, these veterans left those countries behind at the end of their tour of duty and returned home. However, those countries and the experiences did not leave *them* behind as they continue to deal with physical, mental, and emotional damage incurred during their deployment. They are the wounded of our nation.

People say, "Time heals all wounds." For many veterans this is not an accurate statement. Often deep scars remain, and, while time has perhaps softened the agonizing pain, the memories remain and surface with reckless abandon. In addition, in many circles the military is not viewed as a highly regarded calling. For those who gave of themselves for their country, the lack of respect and harsh judgment is difficult to reconcile.

One Quilt of Honor recipient, a Vietnam veteran, poignantly shared, "I never felt appreciated when I came home. No one ever said, 'Thank you for your service, and I'm glad you're home.' Receiving the quilt was like a personal, special thank you just for me."

Over the years the Threadbearers have delivered hundreds of quilts to our veterans—as many as 123 in a given year. These quilts are gifts. No compensation is requested or expected. These ladies have never had a fundraiser to purchase materials and supplies, no raffle or offering plate. And yet thirteen years later, they happily sew away.

What is a gift from the heart? How does it differ from other gifts? A gift from the heart does not focus on the object given but the origin of it. It can be anything—something purchased or handmade, a gift of time or assistance. Personal and treasured, no dollar figure can be placed upon it.

Coming from the mind of God, beginning as a single seed of thought, the basis of it is love, as He is love. Given to one to fulfill, it has a life of its own, continuing to grow over time. These are not gifts that are soon forgotten, ending up in a discard or donation pile. No other type of gift, regardless of its monetary value, has that capability of growth.

A gift from the heart is one that touches not only the recipient but the giver as well. These quilts are a perfect example, providing both physical and emotional comfort for the recipients while giving the ones who bestow the gift a deep sense of satisfaction and purpose.

When it comes time for a Quilt of Honor to be "given a home," as the gifting is called, a small group of women, the ones who have spent hours at the fabric store, the cutting table, and then their sewing machines creating it, gather together and pray. They ask that God be honored, that He is given all gratitude and appreciation. They pray also for the one who will receive the gift.

Following the lead and the example of their heavenly Father as He freely gave and continues to give, these are the Threadbearers, ordinary women with fabric, needle, and thread. Impacting countless men and women, their families, and their friends, these Quilts of Honor are undeniably gifts of love, gifts from the heart.

> Every good gift and every perfect gift is from above,
> and cometh down from the Father of lights.
> —James 1:17 (KJV)

On Gifting with Rules

Rule #1 reads as follows: "This is yours, but it is not yours to keep."

When the plan of gifting money to my five grandgirls, with conditions and terms, was initially planted in my mind, my goal was to encourage them to think beyond themselves. I hoped this would make their Christmas holiday more than just their personal wish lists. Given with the charge of that first rule, the gift that was not theirs to keep provided the opportunity for that experience.

Yesterday was Thanksgiving Day, and today is called Black Friday, commonly viewed as the official beginning of the Christmas shopping season. No time is wasted as consumers are lured out in the wee hours of the morning for great bargains and amazing deals. Thanksgiving dinner has barely had time to digest before shoppers are beckoned to begin purchasing their Christmas gifts, with some stores opening as early as five on Friday.

Gifts and Christmas go hand in hand. In fact, it's quite impossible to think of the holiday without compiling a list with ideas of gifts to be purchased and given to family and friends. For those of the Christian faith, the argument is that the birth of Christ was a gift from God to the world. Therefore, we should gift one another as we were gifted.

For others, gift-giving carries with it the notion of generosity and good will toward one's fellow man. The idea is that at this time of year, peace and love will reign if we put forth the effort to be kind to one another, which is characterized by the giving of gifts, time, and money to others, including charitable endeavors.

As a culture, we are locked into a tradition, and part of that tradition includes presents under a tree to be opened either the night before or the morning of December 25. Christmas without gifts is almost beyond comprehension.

Perhaps you have your own harrowing experiences as to how

quickly the peace and harmony dissipates once the wrapping paper is ripped off and presents are opened, especially if children are involved. Overstimulation, the hype, and anticipation often result in meltdowns as the holiday season culminates in the great unveiling of the gifts. And the same thing can be said for adults as well, as the spirit of Christmas peaks and then enters a crash-and-burn state.

The entire Christmas present and gift-exchange scene has been a mental wrestling match for me for many years. I'm never a Scrooge muttering, "Bah, humbug!" but the word *obscene* is my own description upon viewing the sheer quantity of wrapped gifts loaded around my family's Christmas tree. So much expense, time, and energy is spent in preparation for a single day that comes to an end so quickly. And life goes on.

My grandgirls lack for nothing materially. How could I make Christmas about more than just selfish desires? The idea had begun forming several years ago, but I felt some were too young at that point in time to comprehend the concept I wished to present through personal experience.

Four years ago, I proceeded with a scheme, one that has played out every year since and was repeated yesterday. That first year each of my five grandgirls received a check in the mail made out to them along with a letter. The letter began with, "This is yours, but it is not yours to keep." I went on to ask them if they could remember the gifts I had given them the previous Christmas or the one before that. Then I told them the gift check was one I hoped they would remember for the rest of their lives.

Specific instructions followed. They were to either give the money away or purchase a gift and give that away. They—not their parents—would decide who would be the recipient. All the money had to be spent by Christmas, and it could be given to one person or to several, but it had to be used on others rather than themselves.

Christmas Day arrived, and before opening gifts each grandgirl related what she had done with her money. One had chosen to use it to purchase a sweater for an elderly person. No one in the family knew where the idea of giving to the elderly came from; however, it was what she wanted to do, so she did. Another donated to St. Jude's Children's Hospital after being made aware that all children do not have the same kind of healthy body she has. Two sisters put their money together and, along with the help of their parents, gave a little boy a full-fledged Christmas, complete with scooter, new shoes, coat, books, underwear, and socks. Yet another donated hers to a local facility for abused women and their children—a positive life experience for a young teen. How many teens are even aware that abuse takes place in many relationships?

Each year since then, my grandgirls continue to think beyond themselves as they have given to local needy families by providing gift cards to a toy store and a grocery store as well as sharing with a church, Wounded Warriors, and a homeless person. The one stipulation the little one had was it couldn't be a homeless person standing outside Walmart. We have no idea where that came from either, but those were her terms.

Anonymity is important as they are to give without expectation of recognition or acknowledgment. They are to simply give.

Gift-giving should usually be done without conditions, rules, or stipulations, but I feel this is a valid exception. I have no way of knowing what my grandgirls are learning and experiencing as they think of others besides themselves, but I believe it is invaluable. And so on Thanksgiving I pulled out my checkbook and handed out checks to them. They now know it is money that is theirs, but not theirs to keep. Before we begin our gift exchange on Christmas Day, I'll learn how they chose to spend it as they take turns telling what they did with this gift. It's a new family tradition.

> Freely ye have received, freely give.
> —Matthew 10:8 (KJV)

On Selflessness vs. Selfishness

selflessness: n. Being more concerned with the needs of others than with your own needs; self-sacrificing.

selfishness: n. Concerned chiefly or excessively with self and having little regard for others.

Sitting down in my rocking chair with my morning elixir of green tea laced with honey and apple cider vinegar—with the "mother" of course, which is a term used for vinegar that is unrefined and unfiltered—I began what has become my morning ritual of scrolling through various news feeds on my iPad. I have forgotten the merit and value of the tea, honey, and vinegar combination, but I think it has something to do with alleviating stiffness in the fingers. While I refuse to apply the label *arthritic*, it does seem to help a bit.

One of the first articles I read was about a young woman pregnant with twin girls who had an abortion at twenty weeks. One of her justifications for the abortion was that she already had two girls. After reading the details of what is involved in late-term abortions, I found a seething outrage developing within over what I could only view as an act of selfishness.

"Children are a gift. It matters not how they are given." That is my mantra. While some pregnancies may come at inopportune times or under difficult circumstances, they are not mistakes. The little ones, the innocents, are often considered inconveniences, *their* right to life treated as a matter of choice by the mother and society, and they are readily snuffed out and discarded with no value or worth given. I believe life is a gift and should be treated as such.

Almost fifty years ago, I found myself in a place of desperately wanting a child and unable to conceive. If you were to question my heavenly Father, He would no doubt shake His head and rub His ears upon being reminded of that time in my life. The begging, pleading, crying, negotiating, and, dare I say, harassing was endless. Driven by an intense desire with no fulfillment, this was one of the most difficult times of my life.

Fertility drugs were still experimental, but they were presented as an option. Multiple births often occurred when using them, and, after being told of a mother in Australia conceiving nine babies, I declined. My thought was that I had asked God for a baby, not a litter.

It was then the idea of adoption was placed in my mind, and a door opened up for my husband and me. Having stepped through, I've never looked back.

The phone call came from the adoption agency. Our little girl had been born. My thoughts immediately went to her birth mother, the pregnancy, the labor, the delivery she had just experienced, the sacrifice she was making, and the fact that she was going to leave the hospital empty-handed and brokenhearted. I asked God to give her peace. In a time of closed adoptions, where all records were sealed by the courts, I never expected to ever meet her.

Thirty-one years later, I was given yet another gift when my first grandgirl was adopted by this daughter and her husband through the same agency. Times and laws had changed. This was an open adoption, one where the birth mother chose the parents who would provide a home for and raise the child she was carrying. The parties involved agreed they would establish a level of communication and contact as my grandgirl grew up.

My son-in-law served as president of the Oregon Logging Conference for 2015–16. As first lady, my daughter had certain responsibilities. One was to present a charity at a dessert luncheon, with the proceeds from the luncheon benefitting that charity of choice. She chose the Boys' and Girls' Aid Society of Oregon, the adoption agency both she and her daughter, my grandgirl, were adopted through. Her plan was to make a video presentation rather than a verbal one, and she wanted to include all those women in her life who had been part of her very personal adoption experience.

We were to meet for a photo session and dinner. The five of us ranged in age from sixteen to seventy-one. Two birth mothers, two adoptive mothers, and two adopted children connected by a common bond, a thread that wove its way through all our lives—that of adoption. My daughter was the unique one to be both an adoptee and an adoptive parent.

At the restaurant my daughter's birth mother and I were seated next to each other. Birth mother and birth child had met several years earlier, and I had been included, but the encounter was a brief one. As the dinner neared an end, she leaned over to me and whispered, "She's beautiful. You did such a good job raising her." It was then I was able to thank her for the priceless, selfless gift she had given me. I told her of my prayer for her. Yes, she had been given peace. I told her of the first time I held her precious gift and also revealed that I never took for granted the pain she had gone through or minimized how difficult the decision was to give her child to another, never expecting to ever see her daughter again.

The traits of selflessness or selfishness are not ones that can be covered up or hidden. Actions do speak louder than words, and these traits are readily visible—manifest in behavior, actions, and attitudes. Forming a foundation within each one of us, they can be seen and felt by our families and society. At the core of *all* we do, we come from either a place of selflessness or selfishness.

Facing the option of abortion and choosing instead to carry their babies to full term, two women made the ultimate sacrifice—that of giving up their children. Undoubtedly, this was the most difficult decision and act of their lives.

I cannot imagine my life without these gifts. My life and that of my family would have huge holes were it not for this epitome of selflessness. I am eternally grateful to these two and to the One who heard my cries and answered.

I am reminded of the One who asked no more of them than what He Himself gave.

> For God so loved the world that He gave His
> only Son, so that everyone who believes in him
> may not perish but may have eternal life.
> —John 3:16

On Treasure

treasure: n. A collection of valuable things; accumulated stock of money, jewels, etc.; anything that is greatly valued.

The family was attending my eldest grandgirl's dance recital, and it was intermission time. The sparkly grandgirl and I, the one who endears me with the nickname "Old Lady," had returned from a trip to the restroom, and we were waiting for the second half to begin. As I sat down, she planted herself in my lap. Wrapping my arms around her waist, we talked until it was time for her to return to her seat. All the while I was absorbing that point in time, fully aware it might never happen again. In addition to the fact that she is moving, she is growing up right before my eyes, and, in the future, sitting in Grandma's lap in public will carry with it some reservations.

The nine-year-old grandgirl, the "old soul" who is quiet but mighty, called recently. After chatting for a bit, I asked her what she was doing. "Nothing," she said. "I just wanted to hear your voice." Several days earlier she had run up to me and greeted me with a hug, saying, "Gram Gram!" She hugs as gently as a light breeze, patting softly on the back with tenderness. A hug from her carries with it every bit of love she has to give, and it is felt.

Cherished moments such as these nourish the very essence, the lifeblood of a grandmother.

The word *treasure* often specifically refers to the monetary value of a physical object. From the beginning of time people have searched for lost or buried treasure, with grandiose hopes and goals of boundless wealth. In centuries past, it was perhaps gold or precious gems, a sunken ship or cache of money. Obsessed by that quest, entire lives have been completely absorbed, consumed by the dream and prospect of that pot of gold at the end of the rainbow, the pie in the sky, the mother lode. In that state of mind, nothing else matters. Nothing.

Fast-forward to the twenty-first century, and it is not uncommon for one's treasures to be measured in a stock portfolio, a business or investment opportunity, a profit and loss statement, or real estate holdings. While the goal may appear to be different, the compulsion, drive, and fixation on the pursuit of such is the same, and the base never varies—the love of and desire for money.

I am a woman of wealth. Perhaps you would disagree if you were to see me in my beat-up 1997 Ford Ranger pickup. My financial statement and nonexistent stock portfolio would reinforce a position for argument. And yet I am rich.

In contrast to the commonly held view, my personal definition offers another type of wealth not recorded in a ledger account.

treasure: n. That which money cannot buy; priceless; beyond any price, with no dollar value attached. (personal definition)

My life is packed with such treasure—occasions such as those with my grandgirls, unexpected surprises that brighten my day, interactions with those crossing my path, situations and circumstances that give opportunity to thrive and grow. Often they are in the physical as well—a surprise gift of chocolate, vegetables left by my neighbor at my garage door to greet me when I arrive home from work, a handmade card given by my daughter.

I have a private coffer that overflows with relationships—my family, those who surround me and those who are part of my extended family tree; lifelong friendships, reconnections from the past, and new ones that are developing; associations with the clientele in my gardening business who become my friends as we share our lives with one another. Each person in my life is invaluable and enriches it beyond measure.

Perhaps you can relate. If not, my suggestion is to examine the occurrences in the routine of your life with new eyes. We each have our own experiences—varied, unique, personal, and individual. Positive ones may appear out of nowhere and plant themselves deep within our beings, feeding our souls. Often they come in the midst of difficult circumstances and very hard times, but they provide hope, joy, and light—treasures of the intangible kind.

Physical treasures are often locked away in a vault or a safety deposit box. These treasures referenced are tucked away within oneself. They need no key, and they belong solely to the one to whom they are given. Becoming part of the recipient, no other person has access to them; they cannot be touched or taken.

Given the choice between the two, which would I choose? Hands down, I would—and I do—choose the treasure money cannot buy, the kind given by my Creator. Am I wealthy? Once again, I state, "Yes, I am."

And my greatest treasure of all is God Himself.

> Do not store up for yourselves treasures on earth, where moth and rust consume and where thieves break in and steal; but store up for yourselves treasures in heaven, where neither moth nor rust consumes and where thieves do not break in and steal.
> —Matthew 6:19–20

On Love and Being Blessed

blessed: n. Having divine aid or protection or other blessing.

blessing: n. Some kind of divine or supernatural aid.

The pressure-washing job was what I call a hands-and-knees one, a term applied to a chore that is mindless, one conducive for thought. Standing and holding a spray gun for two hours while cleaning a driveway with a power washer falls in that category. While dealing with the task at hand, one also has the opportunity for solitude and introspection.

The fact that my mind could be empty and filled at the same time seems implausible, but that is how it was. I wasn't focused on a particular issue; however, the events of recent days floated through my mind. I mentally reached out to examine various aspects: a thumbs-up approval from a fifteen-year-old grandgirl after reading a blog post I wrote about her; treasured communication from one who is like a second son; lunch with several former high school classmates, some whom I hadn't seen since graduation more than fifty years ago; an invitation to visit sunny Southern California for a weekend in the dead of winter in order to escape the grim, gray fog of the Willamette Valley.

The weather was sunny and warm, an Indian Summer kind of day in early fall. I had sealed the fitting in the spray gun with that stretchy tape plumbers often use, so the spray was directed toward the cement instead of my legs. I found myself feeling filled and fulfilled, with a deep inner satisfaction. My thoughts wandered, going back in time—a long way back.

Life in my twenties was a difficult period of time, one I describe as "a withdrawal from society." Depression has that effect on a person. The resultant malcontent was, in part, due to a search for something more in life. While sounding quite grandiose, it wasn't.

I merely wanted to know the meaning of life, why I had been born, why I was created. My thinking was that if I was putting in the time, I wanted to make it count and have value. I needed to know my existence mattered. The quest was to find purpose, and I was driven in that quest.

A friendship developed with another young woman, a friendship that exists to this day, although we are no longer young. As we talked, I shared with her the doubt that drove me, my knowledge that God did not love me. She was not an atheist. An atheist does not believe in the existence of God. She *knew* He did not exist. She also knew if He did exist, He would be a God of love. I knew there was a God, but I could not be persuaded of His love for me. We came from two completely different camps, and neither of us could be convinced otherwise.

For those of you who parent, you know how impossible it is to prove your love to a child who doubts it. No matter what is said or done, the efforts are futile, the words fall on deaf ears. And that is how it was with me. I demanded repeatedly of God, requiring proof I was loved. I never received the evidence to satisfy.

The driveway was covered with a lot of moss that needed to be cleaned off, so I had plenty of time to think. Doubt has been replaced by the surety of God's love for me. When and how did that change take place within me? I cannot tell you. I do not know.

Love *is*. The force of it, the power, the strength, and the life of it stands. It is not a scientific problem, a hypothesis that needs a series of experiments or tests to verify its validity. God is love. That I now *know*.

The thought came, settling in the substance of my mind. It was not like a leaf in the wind, which whips by then disappears, but, rather, a statement of fact. When helping the grandgirls with homework, preparing for a test, or reviewing math facts, I often tell them, "Answer me with a period, not a question mark." That is what this was—a period. *I am blessed.*

Celebrities and common folk alike often express having been blessed upon receiving good fortune or success in their lives. On the surface, these words sound appealing but come effortlessly, glibly even. They may also be empty and shallow—their true meaning diminished.

I am one who is reluctant to make a personal application of that word or any others with a spiritual connotation. Much of my life was spent repeating the words of my religious upbringing with no substance or a life to back them up. Words are cheap, and I was the poster child bearing that out.

The statement of being blessed, however, has planted itself within, and I have begun viewing my life through that lens. Processing that truth continues as it infuses my being and becomes a part of me.

My life is rich, and it is full—of relationship with my Father, my family, and my friends.

And, yes, my friend and I are now on common ground. We are in agreement that there is a God. And He does love. I am blessed.

> For everyone who asks receives, and everyone who searches finds, and for everyone who knocks, the door will be opened.
> —Matthew 7:8

Chapter 3

In the Garden

Tidbits and Pearls

On Why I Believe There Is a God

There are some whose belief in the existence of God is affirmed after witnessing the birth of a child. For others it is viewing firsthand the power of the sea, the grandeur of the Grand Canyon, the majesty of Mount Everest, or the vast scope of the Sahara Desert. Then there are those who come to that belief as the result of an epiphany experience, a revelation, or a dream. Some arrive there upon hitting a personal rock bottom with no place else to go or no one to turn to but Him. While I appreciate all those persuasions, my argument for God is confirmed by my gardening equipment experiences.

The *season* has begun. This is just another way of saying that fourteen inches of snow has melted, grass is growing, roses and other shrubs need to be pruned, weeds have erupted, and gardens are waiting to be tended. It also means that the gardening equipment, which has been stored since last fall, needs to be brought out of mothballs and put to use. Such was the case today when my lawn-mowing schedule began in earnest. After loading up the mower, the blower, and the trimmer, which is used for edging, I headed out.

On the jobsite, when I completed the mowing, I removed the trimmer from the back of the truck. It had been several months since I had used it, and I had not winterized it properly, emptying it of fuel before placing it in storage. That, in and of itself, spells a recipe for disaster. After priming it and setting the choke, I began pulling on the starter—and pulling and pulling and pulling.

And this is where my argument for God's existence enters in. I heard myself say, "Please, please, please, God. Please start it." This was a typical reaction for me when dealing with an obstinate piece of equipment. Reminiscent of the Count on *Sesame Street*, I have a habit of counting the number of times I've attempted to start a stubborn machine. By the time I got to thirty, I had decided I wouldn't do any edging. That was when it kicked in. The engine revved, and it was ready to go. Trimmer in tow, off to complete the job, my response was one of thanks.

In all honesty, there have been plenty of times when my equipment didn't start, and my behavior was not one of appreciation and gratitude. The nasty words and attitude, the rants and raves don't even faze Him. He smiles, pats me on the head, and sends me on my way to my equipment people, a gift from Him. Their presence in my life adds to my argument for God.

I would never minimize or negate another's experiences or personal position regarding God. I, too, recognize His work and His hand in new life, nature, and events in the lives of each individual. But, for me, today the proof came through loud and clear. He was three for three—the mower, the blower, and the trimmer. They were all at the ready when needed.

On Weeds

weed: n. Any plant regarded as unwanted at the place where and at the time it is growing.

I weeded Bruce's garden pathways for the hundredth time today. While that is an exaggeration, it wasn't the first time they were weeded. Nor would it be the last. A most rude awakening came when I began my gardening business, The Traveling Gardener. I returned to a client's garden and discovered that the pristine state I had left it in a week or two prior had become an area overridden with weeds. I had honestly expected to find it the way I left it. Perhaps that is the definition of living in denial.

One of my clients is of the thought that a weed is a misunderstood flower. Not me! My feeling is that there is no such thing as a good weed and all weeds are categorized as nasty—briars, ivy, and morning glory alike—and all those that blanket a space, regardless of their size. Each season manifests a different variety, which fills fertile soil, nestling amongst beds of perennials or filling bare spots with a carpet of green.

Growing in the most desolate of soil as well, appearing in crevices in sidewalks and driveways even, weeds come in uninvited—blown by the wind or hitchhiking on birds, cats, dogs, or other critters. Leave a single weed unchecked, and it will spread its seeds as though it were the only plant left in civilization and needed to propagate the earth. It is said a weed seed can lie dormant in the soil for as long as sixty years. While not all are triggered by digging and light, as we dig in the soil we may actually be cultivating them, exposing them to the warmth of the sun, creating an environment for the growth of our worst enemy.

In the simplest of terms, weeds choke out life. They are not plants that coexist but ones that suffocate and inhibit the growth and development of neighboring flora. One can't ignore weeds, or the weeds come out on the winning side. They must be dealt with and constantly kept in check, or they will engulf all that is lovely. In the war on weeds, eradication is always a top priority.

In addition to our physical gardens, each of us has a garden within us. Residing in the inner self, this spiritual garden and the fruit of what grows within cannot be hidden. For example, if bitterness, anger, jealousy, or greed is growing within, it will show in the way our life is lived. When those things of the flesh are dealt with, including idolatry, lack of sexual restraint, quarreling, and dissensions, the fruit of the Spirit is manifest—love, joy, peace, patience, kindness, generosity, faithfulness, gentleness, and self-control. The care and tending of this garden is more important than tending any other area in our lives.

How can we tend something that is invisible? The very essence of our spiritual self is not something we can reach out and touch, yet nothing is more real. Personally, weeding my inner self begins with the acknowledgment that a need exists. Next is the concession I am unable to take care of it on my own. The One who created me is a Master Gardener as well. He knows what needs to be taken care of. He knows how to do it, and He does it well. He actually specializes in the elimination of those things that would stifle and overtake life.

Any garden large or small, which has been lovingly maintained, offers a feast for the eyes and brings joy to the soul. Free of competition from wayward growth, this garden begs to be experienced and savored. So it is with one whose inner garden has been nurtured by the Master. The proper pruning, cultivation, development of the soil, and removal of undesirable vegetation all provide the habitat for *fruit* that is enriching and beneficial to all. Living life surrendered to Him is an attainable and worthwhile goal.

Christ spoke of seeds and weeds in a parable. Grain seeds were sown in a patch of thorns where they were quickly choked out. He explained that the seeds are the Word. "Those sown among the thorns: these are the ones who hear the word, but the cares of the world, and the lure of wealth, and the desire for other things come in and choke the word, and it yields nothing" (Mark 4:18–19).

In a spiritual garden as in a physical garden, weeds cannot be neglected, and eliminating them is always the goal. Those who submit to the work and the handiwork of God are both blessed and a blessing.

May your garden flourish with life and love at the touch of our Father's hand.

On Hikes, Chainsaws, and Limitations

limitation: n. The act of limiting or the state of being limited; a restriction; a boundary, real or metaphorical, caused by some thing or some circumstance; an imperfection or shortcoming that limits something's use or value.

In a blunder of sorts, I had inadvertently scheduled my flight home for early evening rather than early morning, giving me an extra day to spend with my Idaho family. "Would you like to go for a hike?" my daughter asked. "We have time."

"Sure. I'd love that," I responded. It was a perfect fall day—not too hot, not too cold—and I had packed the proper shoes in anticipation of such an activity.

As we neared our destination, my daughter pointed out the foothills we were about to climb. If there was any question as to my ability to make the climb, it was never mentioned. Had the possibility been raised, a seed of doubt would have been planted in my mind, and I would have contemplated my own capability, considering how a stranded seventy-two-year-old woman could be transported off a slope.

Limitations are like that. Doubt coupled with fear creates a virtual cage, a mental and emotional enclosure where we take up residence and live. The barbed-wire barrier of a prison isn't even needed, as life is lived within the seeming comfort of the restrictions we place upon ourselves.

Like an old, well-worn sweater or pair of shoes, comfort is familiar but not necessarily ideal. A personal experience reinforced that very point.

Operating a chainsaw is far too dangerous and should be left to loggers of the male species. At least, that is what I had told myself repeatedly for as long as I can remember. I not only believed it, I *knew* it.

Snow and ice from a recent storm had caused major tree damage.

Chainsaws were buzzing all over the place, though not in my hands—that is, until an opportunity arose.

A client contacted me, asking if I could clean her yard of fallen debris. Some large oak branches had come down and needed to be cut up and removed. Heading over with my pruning saw and long-handled lopper in tow, it didn't take long for me to realize the job would never get done with those tools. It was time to bring out the electric chainsaw.

In my mind, using an electric chainsaw wasn't threatening, whereas a gas-powered one terrified me. Upon tackling the job, however, I realized that, while I was not afraid, an electric chainsaw that cuts through four-inch-diameter oak limbs is every bit as dangerous as a gas-powered one.

Pushed out of my comfort zone and zipping through the branches with my newfound skill, I found myself thinking, *What other limitations have I placed on myself without even realizing it?* I make statements and go about my daily life living in a false perception.

For example, I say, "I don't know how to swim because I don't like water." The truth is fear has taken over, so I never learned. I say, "I can't back a trailer," so I make a point of never pulling one. How hard would it be to take the time to master that skill? I say, "I can't dance," and, therefore, I don't dance. A pattern emerged—that of beginning with a negative, filing it in the mental box called my mind, and continuing on with life, tacitly accepting it as a valid, unchanging, and absolute description of myself.

I was created to have an abundant life, not one marked by self-imposed limitations at every turn. God is always ready to provide opportunities for personal expansion and growth. It is in my hands to accept or reject them.

Hiking up hills and operating a chainsaw are freeing experiences, breaking down the barriers of personal limitations.

And the view is great.

I have come that they may have life, and have it abundantly.
—John 10:10

On Leaving Your Mark

leave your mark: v. To have an effect that changes someone or something (Cambridge Dictionary).

Designated a historical landmark, the small law office carries the name "The Skinner House," the surname belonging to Eugene Skinner, the original founder of the city of Eugene, Oregon. While the front of the building displays a large covered porch with wide steps inviting entry, the back harbored a stark, weed-laden area filled with gravel.

    A personal bonus in my job as a gardener is that work efforts are quite apparent. The appearance of my work space often shows a visible improvement after I complete a job. This back area offers a perfect example. The contrast of the finished work when compared with the way I found it could not have been more evident. I created a narrow bed adjacent to the foundation and bordered it with smooth, melon-sized stones. Planted with succulents and drought-tolerant plants for summer bloom, the space was transformed with color—the bright orange of California poppies and purples of a hearty, wild bloomer.

    Providing a morning greeting, a feast for the eyes for the ones who work there, I couldn't resist the temptation to bring in some spring color as well for the season six months away. The daffodils have faded; however, that bed is now filled with tulips, and the colors are stunning. The bulbs, planted without the knowledge of the employees, provided a welcome surprise—an exclamation point at the end of a dreary winter. I guess it could be said I left my mark.

    We all leave a mark in this life, and not necessarily the kind just referenced. It may be planned or deliberate. More often it is unintended. It might be a positive one, but it could be negative. Leaving one's mark isn't about making a casual impression either. Rather, it's about having an influence with a long-term effect on others. This affects another's life in such a manner that the person is not the same after the encounter, the contrast as real as before-and-after photographs.

Recently, I was told of a grandfather who left such a mark—a positive one. He didn't do anything unusual or out of the ordinary, but the impact of the kind of person he was lives on. The way he lived his life with kindness, acceptance, inclusion, and love has never been forgotten by a grandson. I doubt this grandfather had any idea that decades later his mark would be felt along with the desire to emulate him.

Where and how we leave our mark is personal and individual. For some, it may be through family or in social and business contacts. For others, the goal may be relative to concerns of the environment or planet. For another, it may be like that grandfather, in the day-to-day living of life and the encounters and relationships that develop.

Personally, my goal is of a spiritual nature. My hope is to leave a mark that continues for all eternity. "That's lofty, egotistical even," some might say. Others may comment, "It makes no sense." While some may feel that way, the reality is I have been given one life to live. My desire is for my life to have significance, to have value and purpose. My aspiration is that in living my life, others may see God and seek Him out for themselves.

And so I will continue tending lawns and gardens by mowing, blowing, and edging. I will weed like there is no tomorrow and rake mountains of fallen leaves. I will deal with blackberries and ivy and address a to-do list that never ends, leaving my mark as a gardener.

My true goal, however, is to leave an invisible mark, one not seen with the physical but with the spiritual eye, a mark that is eternal.

It's the Obvious That Will Get You

obvious: adj. Easily discovered, seen, or understood; self-explanatory.

I got a new power washer Sunday, my third within the past year. The first two had been returned to the place of purchase and replaced. When initially filling the gas tank of the first one, gas poured out onto the driveway. The second had a strange odor when it first fired up, made an odd sound, and died. My hope was that this one would function correctly. You may wonder why I continue replacing them with the same type. As long as the store where it was purchased refunds my money with no questions asked and gives me a new one, why not? And as my mother would say, "The third time is a charm."

Since this is my third machine, I am not a newbie but a veteran at assembling them. As is typical, it comes in a large box, and the consumer puts the washer together. Filled with confidence, I briefly perused the instruction sheet, assured I knew what I was doing. There's not much to it—fill it with oil and gas and attach the handle. The next step is to connect one end of a length of flexible tubing to the machine, the other end to the spray wand. Attach a garden hose, turn on the faucet, and one can be power-washing within minutes.

The only step left was to attach the tubing to the spray wand. There was a blue plastic piece on the end of the tubing, and I assumed it was to connect to the wand, but it would not fit. Matching the two proved impossible. After multiple efforts with no success, I finally decided I would wait to make another attempt when I was more alert. The task had become daunting and was worthy of my best efforts. After feeding my brain and my body and getting a good night's sleep, I would try again. It is a verifiable fact that one cannot put a round peg in a square hole, and it seemed as if I had been trying to do that.

The next morning, I was ready to tackle it again. After checking the picture on the instructions, I resumed my effort. Nope. Nada. It wasn't going to fit even when I was rested. Options began floating through my mind. I could return it to the place of purchase to exchange it for machine number four. I could take it to my power equipment repair shop and see if Scott could make it work—Scott can make anything work. Or I could have my son-in-law stop by—I knew he could fix it.

Then the blue piece caught my eyes. It wasn't a connector at all but a screw-on cap, a new feature from the previous two. Voilà! I unscrewed the cap and readily attached the tubing to the spray wand.

Now, here is my point. How obvious was that? It wasn't a secret. It didn't take any special technique or brain skill. It wasn't made deliberately difficult. It was right there all the time. I just missed seeing it until I actually looked and gave it some thought.

So it is with God. He has placed within human beings the fact that He exists. Some will deny that truth. Some say they will accept that truth if and when certain conditions are met. Some will casually treat that truth as though He is part of a giant fairy tale when, in fact, this is His world and we are His creation.

In my life, He is obvious. I see Him in my daily encounters and experiences. I see Him in times of frustration and times of joy and pleasure. I see Him in my inadequacies and my fears, my accomplishments and my courage as He walks with me through life.

My message is: "Look. Open your eyes and see. Look at a flower, the perfection of a baby, the cycle of the seasons, the stars in the sky, the life in the sea. Look at your own capabilities to function, to think, to reason, to laugh, to love, and to live. Look. Open your eyes and *see*."

It's the obvious that will get you every time, whether it's a blue screw-on cap or something that is as plain as the nose on your face—and that would be God.

People will either acknowledge Him in the present or face-to-face later. Sooner is definitely better than later. And while one can say, "I did not believe," one can never say, "You did not show me. I did not see. I did not know."

> For what can be known about God is plain to them, because God has shown it to them. Ever since the creation of the world his eternal power and divine nature, invisible though they are, have been understood and seen through the things he has made. So they are without excuse.
> —Romans 1:19–20

Don't Count the Barberry Shrubs

My gardening business is in its twelfth season, and I know better, but I did it anyway. Pruning the barberry shrubs has been on my to-do list for quite some time. My clients have been away for six weeks and asked me to complete the work before they return. That deadline is less than a week away. What have I done that I shouldn't have? I counted the number of barberry shrubs needing to be pruned.

Most of my work is gratifying. There are, however, two tasks I have encountered that I dread. The first is dealing with ivy. As a first job in my fledgling business, I was asked to remove a mass of ivy. Its far-reaching tendrils had found their way into the interior of the home and needed to be removed at the source. The damaged knuckle on my index finger from trying to remove that stubborn ivy is a reminder of its tenacity.

The second distasteful job is dealing with barberry shrubs. Aptly named, since their branches are covered with barbed thorns, I often wonder if a plant such as this was used to create the crown of thorns for Christ. It is not a friendly shrub. Even while wearing leather gloves, the thorns, which are barbed like fishhooks, penetrate fingers and knuckles. In an attempt to remove a thorn, the barbed end breaks off, remaining embedded, and it takes several weeks before it surfaces. Shearing the shrubs is not an option, since the client requested a more natural look, so each individual branch must be pruned.

As a kid, summers were spent picking row crops in the fields of local farmers—strawberries, raspberries, and beans. If you've ever seen a field of berries or beans growing, you know how long the rows are. I once asked my brother to speculate on the length, and he answered, "Too long," which says it well. For anyone, especially a child, reaching the end of the row and completing its collection of fruit or veggies is an overwhelming prospect. My approach in dealing with the intimidating assignment was to never look up, which made it somewhat manageable.

As a gardener, using that same method when asked to weed a large garden bed, rake a mountain of leaves, apply bark dust or dirt, or deal with a work list a mile long makes completing those gardening tasks feasible as well. Unfortunately, I did not apply that method when pruning the barberry shrubs.

Practicing a similar attitude in daily life is effective also. Each of us faces projects or situations in life that are massive and overwhelming. Perhaps it is planning a move, a wedding, or a trip. It could be preparing for retirement or creating a place for a new child coming into the family. It could be facing a pending surgery or beginning a new job. Even dealing with a weekly schedule for a family can be difficult as homework, social activities, sports practices, games, dance or music lessons, and more fill the hours after school. And then there are the meals.

The old-timers used to say, "Just keep your nose to the grindstone." The origin is said to go back to the days when tools were sharpened on a stone and there was a need for the one doing the sharpening to stay close to the stone while applying pressure. The message is that we should remain focused on the task at hand.

Every journey, every enterprise, no matter how large or small, begins with a single step. If you meet and address the situation, moving forward a step at a time, the whole of it won't mentally swamp you. If you look ahead, many of life's situations do have the potential to wipe you out before you even get started. Case in point: thirty-one barberry shrubs. Thirty-one. I counted them.

The pruning is almost completed. I have four left. This job would not have been so insurmountable if I had applied the wisdom of my childhood. The length of time it has taken me to get it done is a stark indicator of my not adhering to my own philosophy. I would like to think that the next go-round I will practice what I preach, that I will simply tackle the job and move forward without looking ahead at how much is left to do. I'm not offering any promises or guarantees on that one, though.

On the Weather

weather: n. The short term state of the atmosphere at a specific time and place, including the temperature, relative humidity, cloud cover, precipitation, wind, etc.

Elaine said it was going to rain today, I thought as I headed to the truck for a raincoat. Elaine is a gardening client who keeps track of such things, even on an hourly basis. I don't. My tack is to deal with the weather at hand at the moment. I keep two sets of rain gear in my pickup, and my rule of thumb is when both sets are soaked through and I have begun to feel good and wet underneath, then I call it a day. That doesn't say much about the quality of the rain gear I have, does it?

The day was a typical mid-spring one in Oregon's Willamette Valley. I usually comment on the weather at this time of the year by saying, "Of course, it's softball season." Two of my daughters played softball, and anyone who has been around softball, baseball, soccer, track, golf, or lacrosse during an Oregon spring understands. The day can begin with sunshine and blue skies only to have the wind come up, the skies darken, and rain or even hail pelts down. That's what happened today. As I finished my weeding job while wearing my rain gear, I began planning the rest of my day. I mentally listed tasks to do inside, only to turn around and find the rain had stopped. The skies were clear once again.

Weather is a great equalizer, a universal experience. It knows no race or creed and does not recognize class, status, or financial statements. Every corner of the globe is subject to its variances. When a tornado or hurricane, tsunami or flash flood, heat wave or blizzard passes through, the wealthiest men are affected as are the most impoverished. The weather is unbridled, controlled by neither man nor woman.

In naïveté, there was a time when I thought farmers must be

the godliest of men as their very livelihood is so dependent upon the weather. Surely, they would turn to the One who is in control of their destiny. The proper amount of rain and sun is necessary in growing any kind of crop. Too much of either or a lack thereof spells disaster. At this point in my life, I doubt those who provide our food are any more God-fearing than any other group of businessmen, and I would guess there haven't been any studies to reinforce or dispute that thought. My suspicion is that faith depends upon the individual, not the calling.

Shedding myself of my raincoat yesterday and heading off to yet another mowing job—in the sunshine, no less—I thought of the name applied to the One in charge of our weather, that of Mother Nature. In my curiosity I wondered if God ever gets tired of being so labeled and wants to throw His hands up in disgust, if He ever wants to shout, "Do you not see that it is I? I am not a contrived picture, a description created to satisfy your narrow world and your narrow minds!" I would certainly react that way. But, then, that's me. By the way, before the day was over, there was such a deluge of hail that the ground turned white. God, not Mother Nature, put in a busy day weather-wise. Of course, it's softball season in the Willamette Valley.

> For he makes the sun rise on the evil and on the good,
> and sends rain on the righteous and the unrighteous.
> —Matthew 5:45

On Debt

debt: n. Money that one person or entity owes or is required to pay to another, generally as a result of a loan or other financial transaction; the state or condition of owing something to someone.

My clematis is in full bloom, the vine reaching up and spilling over the fence, its large purple blossoms resembling velvet. It is a beauty, one of four taken from a client's garden when he asked that they be removed. Of those four which found their way into my own garden, this one is my favorite.

This same client refused to pay me for work rendered, asserting I had taken too long to bill him. No argument or defense can be offered because he was correct. At the end of a long gardening day, invoicing is often postponed, and I was negligent in billing him in a timely manner. In spite of my procrastination, though, a pretty tidy chunk of change was owed for work done in the heat and dust of summer, satisfying the criteria of debt.

A debt is owed to another; it is an obligation. Perhaps it is money owed for a service provided as in completed gardening work or for a product purchased. Some view indebtedness as the result of personal assistance given or received, whether it's physical, spiritual, mental, or emotional, with no monetary compensation in play. For example, the phrases "I owe you" and "I owe you big time" are often heard when aid is given.

Personally, I choose not to live my life by a balance sheet where assets and liabilities are tallied and kept track of. Given those conditions, I feel the sincerity and purity of a kind deed or act is negated. A favor should not be treated as a business transaction with repayment expected or required.

My former client moved to New York, and he was entered in my tax records as a bad debt. I think of him occasionally when my clematis are in bloom. While I don't carry a grudge or harbor any animosity, I do remember him and the debt he walked away from. My gardening business is now in its twelfth year, and he is the sole client who openly refused to pay. Sometimes I wonder what has happened to him, how his life has gone, and whether it was worth it to dodge an unpaid debt. What a sad statement of a life to have left this mark!

How one lives life matters since impressions and impacts are made on the lives of others, either positive or negative.

A friend wanted to appear at his front door and introduce himself to this client on my behalf, seeking payment. Others suggested he be turned over to a collection agency. I respectfully refused those options. I believe a higher justice is in play and by unequivocally refusing to pay a debt, this man placed himself in a higher court, one where he no longer answers to The Traveling Gardener but to God.

Make no mistake—the collection will be made, and justice will be served.

> Owe no one anything, except to love one another.
> —Romans 13:8

> Beloved, never avenge yourselves, but leave room for the wrath of God; for it is written, "Vengeance is mine, I will repay, says the Lord."
> —Romans 12:19

On Wasps in the Garden
Part 1: Good News

The backyard of the hillside lot where I headed to work is large and deep. The back edge of its lawn butts up against a very steep bank, which connects with the property behind it a street level above. Difficult to maintain, the owner allows ivy to grow on the bank, hoping to have a blanket of ivy instead of wild grasses. Wild blackberries, however, are competing for their space as well, and it is my annual task to cut back the briars, encouraging the ivy to take over. Since it is one of my least favorite gardening tasks, I tend to postpone the job, and this year was no exception. Procrastination, however, does reach its limits. I finally made the decision to tackle them and headed up the bank with pruners in hand.

It was bound to happen sooner or later, I thought. A person can't go traipsing through the brush and dried vegetation like I do without expecting to run into the nasty buggers. I'm talking about another encounter with wasps. It is, after all, that time of the year when wasps become even more temperamental, antisocial, and downright vicious than usual.

Wasps and bees are not one and the same. Their similarities begin and end with the fact that they are both flying insects with the capability of stinging.

Honeybees are mild-mannered and social, living in large colonies. Not only do they pollinate one-third of the food we eat, they also produce honey in their hives for themselves and for human consumption as well. If a honeybee stings a person, it is a defensive reaction, never an offensive one.

Wasps, on the other hand, are naturally a more aggressive predator. There is nothing passive about them. Whereas honeybees use pollen as a source of protein to feed their offspring, wasps procure meat for their larvae. In my opinion, this classifies them as carnivores.

By the end of summer and the beginning of autumn, the wasp workers have nothing left to do. They have fulfilled their mission of providing insects to feed the young grubs back in the nest. Their food of choice is often decaying fruit rather than the protein they eat early on, and they handle nature's wine in the same manner many humans do. They become mean drunks. In addition, the queen has stopped producing the hormone that keeps the wasp colony within the nest. They are on a final binge since these workers will die when the weather turns cold. To say they are not nice is a gross understatement. Behaving with a definite spirit of aggression, they have no problem expressing themselves in an attack-and-conquer fashion.

Wasps have the advantage. Their nests are often hidden, tucked away underground, invisible to the naked eye—a virtual land mine—and they know where we humans are long before we find them.

Last season I drove my weeding tool straight into a wasps' nest buried in the ground. Instantly, my hand, forearm, ankle, and lower leg were covered with them as they stung ferociously. When one swats at a wasp, a chemical is emitted within fifteen seconds, a signal of distress, and those in the nest respond. They swarm, attack, and even chase. Unlike honeybees, which sting once then die, a wasp can sting repeatedly, so the potential for an allergic reaction is ominous.

My body reacted to the sheer quantity of venom. My breathing wasn't affected, but my heart was pounding. Within a matter of minutes, I had a full-blown case of head-to-toe hives.

I recovered from that onslaught, but it was not an event I wished to repeat. While Al-Qaeda and ISIS are definitely terrorist groups, these tiny black-and-yellow stinging critters have the capability of striking their own kind of terror. The mere thought of them caused me to cringe. Fear sat on my shoulder as I set off to do the necessary work on the bank.

I had clipped two or three blackberry vines when I felt something bothering my foot. Looking down, I saw several of my least favorite insects flying around my feet. Glancing up, I saw the hole in the ground less than a foot away, and the wasps swarming out of it. Given my experience the previous year, my composure was impressive.

I walked calmly down the hill—yes, calmly. When a distance away, I killed the two left on my foot. One was trapped between my shoe and my sock, so he was stinging over and over again. I got in the truck, where I have a beesting kit, and headed home, conscious of my breathing and how my body was reacting.

Often situations are described in terms of good news/bad news. This experience, however, was only good news. Yes, I was stung, but the good news was that my body did not go into shock. While I have no desire to meet up with a swarm of wasps again, it is good to know I was able to continue breathing normally and did not break out in hives. My response to the initial assault was a gift. Typically, I would become hysterical, swinging for all I'm worth. I did not step on that nest, which was additional good news. Had I gone up the hillside at a different angle, I would have stepped right on it.

My life is not in my hands. Once again, my heavenly Father was watching over and taking care of me. While I continue to be apprehensive at the thought of wasps and my foot swelled like a football, not a morsel of this encounter was negative, only positive. The day ended with good news.

It goes without saying that the blackberry briars are still up on that bank. I think I'll wait for cooler weather . . . and for my client to have the nest destroyed.

Part 2: On a Return to the Scene

It had been three weeks since I'd mowed. After encountering the wasps' nest on the bank filled with blackberries and ivy, I had postponed the mowing job since I was uncertain what kind of nearby activity might set them off. My client had called in a professional to dispose of the nest, and she notified me that she checked several times and saw no sign of them.

As I unloaded the mower from the truck, I found myself thinking that I was returning to the scene of the crime. While no crime had been committed, I *was* returning to a scene, one which evoked unpleasant memories.

I found myself checking out of the corner of my eye as I mowed past the place where the nest had been located. I had seen several wasps flying around at other sites the past few days, and the cooler weather had dampened their nasty dispositions, so the threat of an attack was past. And yet the memory lingered. I still have not tackled those blackberries up on the bank.

Experiences from our past, some of them from decades ago, have a way of sneaking into the present, influencing not only the way we think but also how we live, holding us emotionally and mentally hostage.

The mind is a tricky beast to try to control. In fact, I'd place it on an equivalency with the tongue when it comes to the degree of difficulty required to discipline it. That's probably why people spend so much money on seminars, books, and videos in an attempt to gain better control over their thoughts and subsequent reactions and their responses to those thoughts. Oh, that it was that easy to simply train one's mind.

Experiences that have caused pain, sadness, turmoil, or grief have the potential to become springboards. Even though that time in our life will probably not be repeated, the memory is often enough to taint the present. It's as though we return to the scene each time a similar situation occurs. I suspect that is why people say to get right back on a horse after getting bucked off, stressing the importance of not allowing a single incident to define one's future. Sometimes that is possible; other times it is not.

So how *does* a person live in the present and not allow the past to color it? How *does* one live without being affected or influenced by those experiences from the past, dealing with a mental recurrence of a difficult time? There is no easy answer because each individual and each situation is unique. My personal experience, however, attests to the effectiveness of dealing with a great One-on-one Counselor, my Creator. He knows me better than anyone else, and healing is possible.

In reflecting on these things, I realized I have an abundance of experiences to draw from that make me an advocate of this approach. I have already lived through more than a few situations which have the potential to ground me and bring me to a screeching halt—except for the work of the One who made me. There are many things from my past that no longer touch me or affect me or my life because of God's hand and His touch. It all takes place in the mind and the inner being.

We—He and I—aren't all the way through the wasp thing yet. I made it through this season with nothing more than a swollen foot and a bite on the neck. I am, however, considering skipping next August and September when the wasps go on their rant.

I am thankful to God, who walks me through these things. I would never make it on my own.

On Hands-and-Knees Kind of Thinking

My clients are in Italy for an extended period of time, and they gave me a list of tasks to do while they are gone. I considered the various chores, which included some pruning, and settled on cleaning up the daylily bed along the front of the veranda. As I began, the thought passed through my mind, *This is a hands-and-knees kind of job. This is when I do my best thinking.* And it is.

When I decided fifteen years ago to live as a single person, it never entered my mind how I would support myself. I soon learned that stating "stay-at-home mom for more than thirty years" on a résumé didn't translate into today's job market, and the fact I had experience in the insurance industry forty years ago wasn't any better.

The owner of a small local nursery called Wild By Nature hired me, giving me the opportunity to grow and to thrive. Working outdoors suited me. I found it the perfect environment. As I tended the plants, shrubs, and trees, the realization eventually came: I was being tended to as well. I was a stronger person when I left that position than when I began.

In the nursery business there is a lot of interaction with people during the busy season, but there are also long stretches of solitary work in the greenhouse or in the nursery itself—watering, transplanting seedlings, taking cuttings, and dealing with a host of stock. It was an ideal setting in which to work as my life was in the process of being renewed and refreshed.

In the gardening world, *hands-and-knees work* is self-explanatory. It is work that can only satisfactorily be done by crawling around on your hands and knees while cleaning out under shrubs, grubbing out errant weeds, deadheading spent blossoms, and removing dead foliage.

The work itself is mindless for the most part, but I find it to be most productive when the time is used for thinking. Distractions are minimal as I focus on the task at hand, the area right beneath my nose. There is no way to speed up the process while doing the job well. It just takes time. Given that scenario, the opportunity is optimal for thought.

While meditation is more conducive to emptying one's mind of thought, the thinking I refer to is more like a pinball machine, where thoughts ricochet like balls, bouncing around before finally landing. There *are* times when my mind is quiet, absorbing the scenery and the sounds around me. Other times it's as though a wrestling match is taking place within as I consider the whys and the things in my life I don't understand. Often a spring cleaning takes place as mental junk is set aside for the trash, never to be considered again. And then there is the time of pure, simple gratitude as I sit quietly before my heavenly Father.

I am a proponent of this kind of thinking for young and old alike, and I would argue that one doesn't have to be on hands and knees, wallowing in the dirt. Each of us has our own personal place where we go when we feel the need to be alone and think. It might happen while driving to and from work, walking on a treadmill or outdoors, sewing, relaxing on a porch or in a boat, folding laundry, or doing daily chores. Mine just happens to include my workplace.

Life is filled with an overload of stimuli—cell phones with texting and Twittering, television with limitless channels, never-ending music. A time of quiet and thought is scarce. Each day is filled with schedules, choices of activities, and busyness. Children are growing up in our society in a raucous state of cacophony, where being alone with one's thoughts is a rarity not the norm.

Some have suggested that I listen to music while I'm performing such mundane chores in order to make the time pass more quickly. I always say, "No, then I wouldn't be able to think . . . really think."

As humans, we have been given the ability to think, to reason, to make decisions. It is a gift we should not squander or relinquish. Besides, who knows what we might find in the recesses of our mind, what problems may be solved, what discoveries made? For me, nothing compares to that kind of thought process, the hands-and-knees kind of thinking.

Try it. You just might like it.

>Be still and know that I am God!
>—Psalm 46:10

On Being in a Superball State

To say I have been in a Zen-like place, calm and at peace with myself and my life recently would be an utter fallacy. In fact, it would be a bald-faced lie. A better description is that of being in a superball state. Superballs are small, bouncy balls. They don't just bounce—they ricochet off every time they make contact with a surface until they are spent and come to a standstill. There is no way to predict where they will end up.

The blackberry vines on the bank had been waiting for me for several weeks. The task of their removal had been postponed after encountering a wasps' nest in their midst. My fear ran deep, even though my client had eradicated the nest. However, decent weather will be coming to an end, and I had run out of reasons or, rather, excuses. The time had come to tackle them.

There is no shortcut, no easy way. It means plowing through the knee-deep ivy they are entangled in and cutting back the rampant, expansive vines at their base one at a time. Then I have to drag them down the hill to a location where they can then be hauled off. The job is an ideal one for forcing me to stop and examine myself.

This is not the first time I've been in a superball state. I have a history of spiritually packing up my bags and heading off on my own when I am confronted with a reality, a truth I don't particularly want to face or don't agree with. In years past this would last for several months before running out of steam and landing back on the very thing I had tried to avoid.

Over time I have gotten better in dealing with issues head-on, yet here it was once again, that erratic state of mind. There are no skipped steps in my life, no playing leapfrog. There is an order. Each step is crucial, and there is no moving forward until I deal with *whatever* it is I am trying to run from.

I recognized that state, the antithesis of peace. So I began questioning what was going on, what was really taking place within.

As I cut back the vines, the mental garbage began to slough off bit by bit. It was a housecleaning of sorts, and I ended up at the place where I had tried to bail.

Quietly, my heavenly Father reminded me that He had recently asked me to "have patience" in dealing with a situation in my life. I responded, "Yeah, uh-huh, sure. Got it." That was right before I took off. And so I ended up in this place of being scattered rather than grounded and focused, all because it wasn't what I wanted to hear.

I am fortunate to have One who doesn't allow me my own way, who guides me with a sure hand, who is adept at clearing clutter and junk out of the way, and who cares enough that He will not let me remain in situations I would regret.

What a deal! The blackberry vines were cleared off the bank, enabling me to cross a job off my to-do list. I received priceless, personal counseling, and I am once again back on track, moving forward instead of bouncing all around like a superball. Now it is just a matter of removing all the blackberry stickers from my fingers.

> I am leaving you with a gift—peace of mind and
> heart. And the peace I give is a gift the world
> cannot give. So don't be troubled or afraid.
> —John 14:27 (NLT)

On the Golden Rule

As soon as I fired up the trimmer and began edging my lawn, my neighbor came out the front door of the adjacent duplex. It wasn't a surprise. In fact, I knew it was going to happen. I knew he was going to ask if I could mow his lawn as well. That is the reason I had spent the previous half hour inside having an inner wrestling match. I had even considered waiting to mow until the next morning after he left for work in order to avoid the encounter.

It is the time of the year when grass has begun growing again, responding to warmer days and longer periods of sunlight. With several days away from home planned for the upcoming week, I wanted to have my lawn mowed before leaving, and I had shortened my workday in order to get that done.

Whereas my neighbor has no lawn equipment, my garage is filled with a variety of tools. As part and parcel of my gardening business, the professional-grade lawn mower is at home in the back of my truck. One would think I would be more than willing to share. One would think. But my resistance was palpable. I clearly did not want to mow his lawn for him.

Giving him a cursory nod, I turned my back on him, wielding the piece of equipment as though the task at hand was the most important thing I had to do since rearing my children. Sure enough, as I finished, he asked how much I would charge to mow his lawn as well. I coolly responded I would mow it for him without payment.

It was therapy time behind the mower, a stark reflection in the mirror placed in front of me.

Am I just a hypocrite? I asked. *One who has only words and no actions to back them up?* I scrolled through a long list of excuses, all of them placing me in a *most* favorable light. They all quickly fell away.

What is commonly known as the Golden Rule came to mind. *Do unto others as you would have them do unto you.* Everything within me was in direct opposition to that instruction.

Back and forth, back and forth, I mowed, feeling quite ashamed of myself yet aware of the inability to change at will.

The nasty attitude began to abate the more I mowed, and this is where I ended: It is so easy to do things for those who are near and dear to *me*—friends, family, favored clients. It's not so easy when it is one I have no relationship with, but one who is near and dear to my Father. He wanted this done for my neighbor, and my mower and I were only tools used to bring it about.

From henceforth, I have no doubt I will mow my neighbor's lawn when I mow mine, and he won't have to ask. It's what I would want done for me if the situation were reversed, and it is what my Father wants.

A lot of processing is still taking place within me. This is a lesson with many ramifications. Life with my heavenly Father is messy at times because I am messy. However, He can clean it up, and it is never without inner growth, progress, and results.

> You shall love your neighbor as yourself.
> —Matthew 22:39

On Self-Pity

self-pity: n. Excessive, self-absorbed unhappiness over one's life; a self-indulgent, exaggerated attitude concerning one's difficulties, hardships, etc.

"Glad to have you back," a reader commented, referencing the fact it had been more than a month since I had written and posted anything on my blog. When yet another one mentioned the same thing, it gave me pause for thought.

I write only what I experience. Where *have* I been and what has been going on in my life for the past month that has kept me from sharing myself?

Today was a mowing day, a wet one at that, but I had plenty of time to think as I plodded back and forth behind my mower. Somewhere between the second lawn and the fourth one, I knew exactly where I had been.

Stuck in the quicksand of self-pity and consumed by a "poor me" attitude, it gave me good reason to look at that state, that place.

When my focus is on myself, life is like a hamster wheel, the scenery never changing, the theme song remaining the same. Self-pity is a debilitating place, rendering one incapable of reaching out to others. It is the equivalent of creating one's own solitary confinement, a self-imprisonment.

The gardening season has been a wet one, with my schedule a bit overwhelming, but no worse than other years. My attitude is what has made life a chore.

"I am old, and I am soooo tired," I kept telling God. "I'm not going to make it." Can you hear the wailing? I'm surprised I didn't resort to weeping and beating on my chest. Only He knows how many times I sounded that cry of desperation, and I imagine He brought out the earplugs.

When I tried dragging a friend along to my pity party, I knew something needed to change, for it had gone beyond whining, moaning, and groaning. I was miserable in my state of negativity.

Finally, I stopped throwing words at God and planted myself before Him in acquiescence.

Softly, quietly, I heard, "In everything give thanks, for this is My will."

I cannot explain to you how change takes place at the hand of our Creator. I only know that it does. *I'm not suffering*, I thought. *I'm just tired.* And that is how I came back. Once again, I am free to share.

I worked today in inclement weather and got quite soaked, and yet the day was a good one, a productive one. That is what it is like when I'm not wallowing in self-pity.

"Our God is a good God," I told my friend. And He is.

On Granny Gear

granny gear: n. The lowest gear on a vehicle.

Dragging my feet, procrastinating, digging in my heels—any way I phrase it, I have been taking my sweet time heading out to work. I know I'm operating with brakes on when I hear myself pleading, "Just get me going, Father. Please."

Making a detour to the backyard to check the raspberries and to graze, the thought occurred: *I'm in granny gear.* It brought a chuckle since that description was so fitting and on more than one level.

Those who learned to drive with a stick shift will understand. And is there any other way to learn to drive than with a stick? If you learned to drive with an automatic transmission, let me explain. Granny gear is the lowest of gears in a vehicle with a manual transmission, a gear in which maximum speed is a virtual crawl.

When I was eight years old, Dad placed me up on the tractor seat and explained to me what to do and how to do it. I can only imagine the scene—a tiny girl on a very large tractor, stretching her legs to reach the pedals. Push the clutch in with the left foot, move the gearshift into granny gear, release the clutch, and begin moving forward. To stop, I was to push the clutch in with the left foot and apply pressure on the brake with my right foot. It was my first driver's education lesson.

My task was to steer the giant tractor through the hayfield while pulling a trailer, stopping periodically for my brothers and Dad to load the bales of hay. There isn't much to run into in the wide, open field other than hay bales, so it was the perfect place to learn how to drive. Plus, operating in granny gear meant I wasn't particularly dangerous or threatening to anyone or anything.

And here I am, all these years later—in granny gear once again. Slow motion has been my *modus operandi* for several months now. This gardening season has been an unusual one for me. Getting into a real work rhythm has proven elusive. When I am operating full throttle, it is not unusual to be on the job site by eight in the morning and return home ten hours later. This year, I find I am puttering around the house, taking my time, and I am fortunate if I make it to a job by ten o'clock. At the other end of the day, there are always a variety of reasons (or excuses) to call it a day and head back home.

When I am able to put circumstances in my life into words, when they can be described, it seems as though I have turned a corner. Situations that have been troubling me are brought into focus, and there is clarity. I have been bothered a great deal by my lackadaisical approach to work and have judged myself as being lazy. The granny-gear description is perfect. Not only am I moving slowly, but I am literally a granny five times over.

My work habits can neither be explained nor understood. I don't have to know why. What I will do is just keep going. And that is a whole other subject for a whole other day. Besides, even in granny gear, one can end up covering a lot of territory (or hayfield). It may take a while, but it's better than standing still. Remember the story of "The Tortoise and the Hare"? I think I've made my point.

On Sparring with a Squirrel

He makes his appearance known every morning, blithely scampering across the top of the fence like a tightrope walker. This little rodent and I have been at war recently. War is probably too strong a term. More like a tug-of-war as he and I spar with one another. While I generally don't class squirrels as rodents, they *are* in the same family.

Let me preface this by stating I am not an animal person. I'm more a people person. I don't have anything against animals. They simply aren't my cup of tea. I can honestly say respect for a squirrel has never been part of my DNA.

The war began when I started a sweeping cleanup of my backyard. One of the projects included dealing with a birdfeeder that had not been in use for quite some time. Unbeknownst to me, wasps had taken up residence inside and built a nest. Of course, I did not realize this until I aggressively turned it upside down and they made themselves evident. Anxious to get my feeder back in working order so I could welcome birds into my backyard, I waited until dark, sprayed wasp spray into the main body, and stuffed the entrances with paper.

As I nursed a sting on my hand, what seemed like a pretty straightforward task had already become complicated.

The next day, with the feeder all prepped and filled with seed, I decided to move it to a location more readily visible from my kitchen window, taking into account the local squirrel's habit of helping himself to the feed as well. I sat back, awaiting the influx of birds. At the end of my workday, I was thrilled to discover evidence that the feeder was effective since birdseed was scattered upon the ground.

And so it continued for several days *until* I happened to be looking out the window when the resident squirrel made his appearance. This little guy was quite the acrobat and could certainly qualify for an Olympic standing broad jump. Leaping a span of several feet from the fence to the feeder, he helped himself without so much as leaving a thank-you note. It was he who had scattered the seed, not any visiting birds.

The tug-of-war began. Intent upon feeding birds, not squirrels, I moved the feeder to another location, not taking into account his ability to scale vertical posts and access the feeder with little effort. He had found a gold mine—food that was readily available—and he took advantage of it immediately.

Once again, I relocated the feeder to a space farther away from the fence. This is when the little varmint earned my respect.

I watched as he made his usual morning arrival, fully expecting to have a meal fit for a king, breakfast on a platter. Stopping, he sat on his haunches, and I could almost hear him thinking, the wheels grinding inside his head. For the longest time, he perched atop the fence, calculating whether or not he was going to be able to reach the feeder by jumping. His human counterparts would have jumped first and fallen splat upon the ground before realizing what had worked before wasn't going to work this time around.

This showed not only instinct but intelligence. I saw it in his eyes. He turned away, off to consider another plan, another approach.

Some believe that the entire world evolved—that it began as a force, developing and changing to what we see and know today. I am not one of those. It is my belief that the world and everything in it, all that we see and know and all that we don't see and don't know, was created by God.

As a gardener, I see what happens around me. There is truth in the adage "Compost happens." Matter always breaks down, returning to its origin. It doesn't become something different. One need only look around at the state of our world and its inhabitants to realize evolution is not taking place.

That little squirrel was created with intelligence to live and to survive in this world, as are we all. Intelligence is but one aspect of being a created being. Personality and individuality are others.

If such care and thought were given to the creation of a small being, how much more was given to the human race, which was created in the image of God? In humanity's effort and desire to control all things, including their destiny, people have forgotten where they came from and the source of it all. They are setting themselves up for failure by not acknowledging or factoring in this most important piece of life.

I do wonder what it is going to take before there is an awakening to the truth.

The little squirrel comes back every morning, checking to see if things have changed and has adjusted to eating seeds scattered on the ground beneath the feeder. In addition to the seed, he helps himself to the apples in my backyard, taking a bite of each before casting it to the ground. I doubt I'll be buying any food to supplement his diet. The tug-of-war continues.

Chapter 4

An Ordinary Life Extraordinaire

On the Gift of Life

life: n. *Existence.*

We each have only one life, and it is a gift we should never take casually but treat with respect. Wrapping the mind around the one-of-a-kind originality of each person can be a mental struggle. As individual, as unique as a snowflake, this profound concept staggers the thinking. Having emanated from the mind and heart of the Creator, every person is important and valuable.

I love my life. It isn't just that I love my work, my interests, my activities, the things that make up my everyday living, even though I do. I love my life. I love *being*. That has not always been the case, though. There was a period in my life—and it covered a very long stretch of time—when I did not want to *be*.

What was is no more. The bleak, hopeless condition of my life no longer exists. Contrast and comparison, ying and yang, black and white, day and night. After living in a state of simply existing for so many years, I appreciate and treasure beyond words the life I now have.

How was the transition made from the one state to the other? It was not in a retreat to the desert or a mountaintop, but in ordinary life I was given the answer to a lifelong question: "Why am I alive? Why was I born, and what is the point of my life?"

He spoke quietly to my heart, "That you might know Me, the one and only true, living God."

God's plan and deepest desire is to have a relationship with those He created. He has given us the choice to accept that or reject it.

He is life, and in Him I found life and was given mine. He is well worth knowing.

> I am come that they might have life, and that
> they might have it more abundantly.
> —John 10:10 (KJV)

On All Things Ordinary

ordinary: adj. Being part of the natural order of things, normal, customary, routine.

extraordinary: adj. Not ordinary, exceptional, unusual.

A former high school classmate commented, "I do love the way you write and make the ordinary so much more."

In a few words, she aptly described my life and how I view the world and everything in it. "The ordinary *is* so much more," I responded.

We live in an age of superlatives—big government and big banks, megachurches, multifaceted products, multibillionaires, superstars, supersized meals, high-speed Internet, corporate farming, conglomerates, all things global. In contrast, the word *ordinary* carries with it a negative connotation, as though something is lacking. Perhaps certain goals have not been set and met. Maybe focus has been lost. Something is definitely askew. How *can* ordinary be a good thing? How can it be optimal and desirable?

Ordinary, however, is what makes up our everyday lives. Quite literally, it is what makes the world go around. Consistent, predictable, and typical, we rely on and expect ordinary, whether we realize it or not. Things that are out of the ordinary give us a jolt, put a kink in our plans, and throw us for a loop.

The sun rises and sets. The seasons change as one flows and melds into the next. Babies are conceived and born. As they grow up, a changing of the guard takes place, and that generation then becomes the next to rule the world. There is birth, and there is death. Life is filled with ordinary things, the various rhythms and cycles meshing together like gears, propelling us all forward into the future, unknown though it may be.

How, then, does ordinary become something more? How does it become extraordinary?

I am reminded of a Bible story.

Christ and His twelve disciples went to a desolate place for a retreat of sorts, a time of privacy and rest. A multitude of people in the thousands discovered where they went and inundated the area, wanting to be healed or delivered from demons, begging to be taught. Recognizing their needs, He did not turn them away.

It became late in the day. With no food available in the remote area, the crowd became hungry. The disciples wanted to send everyone off to find food, but Jesus had a plan. A young boy offered food he had brought—five loaves of barley bread and two small fish, which was probably quite ordinary fare for that time. (Isn't it just like a boy to make sure he has a little snack for himself as he heads out the door?)

The throng numbered five thousand men, and that didn't include the women and children. It was obvious there wasn't a sufficient amount to feed everyone. The disciples pooled their money and quickly realized they weren't even close to having enough funds to purchase food for that many people even if they found some at a nearby village.

Christ accepted the gift of bread and fish from the boy, gave thanks to God, and began giving the food to the disciples to distribute to the crowd. The people ate. They were all filled, and twelve full baskets were left over—from five small loaves of bread and two fish.

Ordinary became extraordinary.

Everything about my life and about me is ordinary—where I live, how I live, the food I eat, the vehicle I drive, the work I do. You could almost set your clock by my morning rising time. I begin each day with a cup of my green tea brew. Then I make a green smoothie concoction of spinach, kale, banana, and orange. I top everything off with a bowl of cereal. While you might not consider the smoothie ordinary, for me it is. My life has a sameness about it, a predictable routine.

And yet in the ordinary, there are times of extraordinary. They come when I least expect them and always fill my soul with the knowledge that my life consists of more than just myself. A conversation with a grocery store clerk who is frightened and frustrated about a family situation; a chance encounter with a neighbor from years gone by while out shopping; a message from a young man who has struggled in life yet stays in contact; a phone call from an old friend I haven't seen in years, thanking me for praying for him—these people open the doors to their inner selves and allow me to enter in.

My life is not my own. I do not know if that is easily understood, but it's the truth. In giving up one's life, doors are opened to experience moments where all that is ordinary becomes extraordinary. That is what happened when that young boy gave Jesus all that he had to give. That is the touch of God in everyday life.

An Oxymoron

oxymoron: n. A contradiction in terms.

It is the nature of people to want to fix things, including themselves. Self-help and how-to books, videos, and audio recordings abound, offering a variety of methods and techniques to bring about personal change within one's life.

As I headed out to begin my workday, the thought passed through my mind: *Always, ever—growing, changing.*

Not all aspire to or desire to change within themselves. I'm not quite sure why that is. Perhaps it is the "old shoe" or "old sweater" syndrome. Living in the status quo *can* become very comfortable. It is also very stagnant and monotonous. Where there is life within, there is change. Change is evidence of life.

How can it be that I have changed so but I am the same? That was the question under consideration as I plowed through weeds with my hand tool. And, then, I saw the truth of that.

Three years ago I purchased a lovely birch tree with maroon-colored leaves. It complements several other shrubs in my front yard, and I am able to see it from where I sit at my computer. Although quite small when I got it, it has grown to at least triple its original size. That tree has changed dramatically, but it hasn't changed at all. The essence of it is still there. Its growth bears out that it is alive and thriving, and that is visible for all to see.

And so it is with me. I am not the same person I used to be, and yet I am.

I am still the little girl who loves Dairy Queen ice cream, who laughs too loudly and finds the volume of my voice increases when I am excited, who enjoys creating things with my hands, who loves sunsets and the smell of babies. I am that person who is competitive, one who delights in helping grandchildren learn.

As I live my life, the change is dramatic. I am far removed from the person I used to be. I am patient where once I was impatient, flexible rather than rigid, and slow to anger instead of quick. I have learned to listen, to talk less, to laugh at myself rather than at others, and to restrain from judging others.

I am a walking, breathing oxymoron. I am the same, and I am different. This is the result of walking step-by-step with God. True change happens only at His hand.

On Identities and the Theft Thereof

identity: n. Difference or character that marks off an individual from the rest of the same kind.

identity theft: n. The deliberate assumption of another person's identity, usually to gain access to that person's finances or to frame a person for a crime.

I find it interesting how we, as humans, go about our everyday lives, never giving a second thought to a whole multitude of subjects, situations, or scenarios—that is, until we turn a corner and find ourselves dealing with one we had neither planned nor expected. These issues may run the gamut from dreadful to exciting, ordinary to momentous. They may be personal, or they could be natural events shared with a community of neighbors, such as hurricanes, fires, floods, or earthquakes. There are those who would say that variety is the spice of life. Or not. Some circumstances are just very difficult and ponderous.

The theft of my purse with all its contents several days ago thrust me into just that kind of a position, putting my mind and my life in a place it had not been before. It certainly wasn't something I had previously considered. As with most people, my wallet contained credit and debit cards and my driver's license. Just that morning I had put both my personal and business checkbooks into the purse. Breaking a cardinal rule, my Social Security card was also tucked away inside. I knew better, but I carried it with me anyway. It was my original and hearkened back to the days when I was a young girl, earning money by picking strawberries, raspberries, and beans every summer. So much for sentiment.

Identity theft has become something other than a term I used to hear about. In the days since the loss of my purse, I have found myself thinking about what that really means.

According to a research study, there were 16.7 million victims of identity fraud in the United States in 2017. The amount stolen that year hit $16.8 billion. While my experience was one of physical theft, thieves have found a gold mine via cyberspace, where personal information is accessed and then used for their own gain.

I am one of a kind, a specialty item, as are each of you. In all of time, there has never been another me. Nor will there ever be. Somewhere in the heavens, there is probably a collective sigh of relief over that one. In my mind's eye, I can see my mother nodding her head in agreement.

Every single thing about me is unique and complex. That is what makes my identity mine and mine alone. Each and every person has his or her own individuality. There are no duplicates. This is mind-boggling—impossible to comprehend with our finite minds.

I have concluded that the term *identity theft* is inaccurate. It is not possible; it cannot happen. The substance, the essence of a person cannot be stolen; no one can take my identity or any other's. Someone stole several things that identify my physical life—the credit cards, driver's license, and Social Security card. But they did not steal my identity. It's not up for grabs.

And for that I am grateful.

> Before I formed you in the womb I knew you.
> —Jeremiah 1:5

> I will praise thee; for I am fearfully and wonderfully made: marvelous are thy works; and that my soul knoweth right well.
> —Psalm 139:14 (KJV)

> But even the hairs of your head are all counted. Do not be afraid.
> —Luke 12:7

On the Things I Have Learned from My Truck

My transportation of choice the past two days has been a gorgeous, gas-guzzling 2014 Chevy Tahoe, the kind of SUV red-blooded males drool over as they discuss horsepower, torque, and God knows what else. This is unlike the reaction my 97 Ford Ranger pickup evokes, which would be none at all.

In all honesty, I can't really say it was my choice. It was the only vehicle available on the car rental lot. They rented it for the same price as the compact car I had reserved, but I'm certain when I refill the gas tank to return the vehicle, that savings will disappear.

It won't be long before the guy at Avis, the rental lot, and I are on a first-name basis. When I walked through the door yesterday morning, he commented, "Is your truck in the shop again?" He nailed it. When problems occur with my pickup, I still need transportation for work, and that is how our relationship has developed.

While heading home from a job the other day, I found myself thinking about surprises. I thought about how we don't know the way any day is going to unfold or what is going to happen. We have so little control over the occurrences in our lives. And then it happened—my very own surprise!

It was rush-hour traffic, so I was driving with all my senses in gear. Out of the corner of my eye, I glimpsed it. It was *the* light. If I didn't know differently, I'd say my little truck was sharing some Christmas holiday spirit, as the "check engine" light shone brightly. Nothing seemed amiss, so I headed on home, knowing I would call Marty, my mechanic, the next morning. My truck has spent so much time in his shop, he and I *are* on a first-name basis.

This truck has been a part of my life for almost twelve years. I have never named it. I couldn't decide whether to attribute a male or female label, so I call it my workhorse. I've clocked more than

140,000 miles on it, and my odometer currently reads more than 225,000 miles. That means the two of us have spent a lot of time together. You could say we have an ongoing relationship, and it has become an old friend. Though an inanimate object, I have learned a lot from my truck, much of which is applicable to those of us who *are* alive and well.

An important lesson is that, just because a lot of highway has been covered and a lot of miles traveled, it does not mean the vehicle is without worth. Granted, my truck isn't capable of participating in a NASCAR race, but there is something to be said about meandering the back roads, taking one's time at a leisurely pace, absorbing and enjoying one's surroundings rather than doing laps at breakneck speed. Yes, it is old, but it's not ready for the scrapyard yet. It still has a lot of life left in it.

Nothing about this truck is perfect, including its exterior, its interior, or under the hood. Each dent and scrape has its own backstory. The gouge in the interior roof liner happened when I was trying to put my hedge trimmer inside and the angle was wrong. The scratches on the paint are from some branches that inadvertently scraped the truck while I was loading them. Then there's the dent on the side where a client's neighbor backed out of the drive across the street and didn't turn in time. I heard it when it happened.

The same can be said of me. While I don't carry wounds of war, the perfect body of infancy has been marked by scars—each one a reminder of the incident causing it. The scar on my knee takes me back to second grade and a fall off the teeter-totter at school. The crown on a chipped tooth reminds me of playing chase on the merry-go-round and coming up the loser. A scar on my eyebrow happened while I was the catcher in a ball game and stood too close to the batter and her bat. They are scars that comprise the story of my life, a virtual nonfiction book.

My truck is well-maintained. Oil changes are performed regularly, belts and brakes checked, tires rotated. I do what I am told to do when it needs to be done—by the Lube-It shop, the tire shop, and the mechanic. I have learned, however, that even with maintenance, parts wear out with time and need to be repaired or replaced. Isn't that true for us as well? Sometimes the body just wears out and breaks down, despite being nurtured and well taken care of.

That brings me to the most important thing I have learned from my little red truck. When the "check engine" light comes on, it must not be ignored. As one of the guys at the shop put it, "It won't repair itself. It never gets better."

We are in that same category. While the body does heal and repair itself, we have those areas deep within that don't, those not visible to the physical eye. Turning a blind eye doesn't make them go away. They don't disappear, and they never get better. They need to be acknowledged and dealt with.

Perhaps you still carry a hurt from childhood. Maybe you harbor anger and frustration over an unresolved family situation. Perhaps you have experienced a fissure in a relationship and the resulting pain. Maybe you've felt grief because of the loss of a friend, whether a person or a pet.

As humans, sometimes it seems easier to push all the feelings inside as deeply as possible rather than confront them or allow them to confront us. That is never the easier way. Nor is it the better way.

While we don't have a "check engine" light that shows up, there are usually indicators of such problems. As with my truck, looking the other way is not a solution. Getting problems out in the light of day, laying them out on the table is a good start. God cannot heal what isn't acknowledged.

When the time comes for me to set aside that 1997 Ford Ranger pickup, I'm not sure how I'm going to feel. I have been holding on to it for quite a while. As with the rest of my life though, I have no doubt I will know when it is time, and I will be ready. Perhaps it will coincide with the completion of this gardening gig. The allure of AC in a replacement vehicle will no doubt help with the transition.

Thank God for the longevity and endurance of Ford Ranger pickups. This experience has been enough to convert me into a "Ford man"—or make that "Ford woman." Add that to the list of the things I have learned from my truck.

It's Been a Good Day

My eyelids grew heavy as I sat and knitted in my rocking chair. Knitting cotton dishcloths is something I've begun doing again. Bringing nearly instant gratification, they are easily finished in a short period of time without much thought involved. My mother taught me to knit as a young girl. The first projects were cotton dishcloths, so in a sense I've gone back to my roots.

The only sounds were of the dryer and a soft whir of the heat pump, with an occasional car driving by outside. A call to a niece had resulted in my message left on her answering machine, so it was just the knitting and me. Thoughts of my day rambled through my mind with no real connection or order.

Earlier, coming into the house at the end of a gardening workday, I heard myself say, "It's been a good day." And, now, as I knitted and rocked, I considered the events of my day.

The day began early at the piano. I have been working on a composition titled "Creation Sings," written by a family member. The music fills me, and I had recorded it on my phone, listening to its beauty throughout the day.

On the way to a work project, I picked up a prescription for a client/friend. Stopping by her home, we chatted and laughed. She is an older person in years yet young in spirit. I like her a lot, and it is always a treat to be around her.

Often when making an assessment of a good day, it pertains to the amount of physical work I have accomplished. And on that one level, today was no different. The home of a former client who recently passed away is being prepared to go on the market. The yard and garden need to be made ready for the sale, so I spent a chunk of the day making that happen. Great progress had taken place as weeds and debris were removed, revealing rockwork and hidden flowering plants.

A young man had been called in to help with the project. While performing this hands-and-knees kind of work, conversation flowed easily. The subject of God came up early in the day. We readily exchanged thoughts and beliefs with interjections of: "It is my belief . . ." "What do you think?" "If I am to understand you . . ." "I disagree with you on that point." In some areas our points of view were quite dissimilar, and yet we shared and laughed, getting to know each other as people.

Going our separate ways at the end of the workday, I thanked him and told him how much I appreciated our time in the garden.

"It is so nice meeting someone who is opinionated in their beliefs and convictions and yet open to listen," he said.

"What is the opposite of that?" I asked.

"Obstinate."

The day came to a close with a text from a grandgirl. "When are you going to be home, Grandma?" She wanted to talk on the phone, and we did. Being told you are loved by a grandgirl makes any day a good day.

My days are very seldom filled with exciting events. *Landmark* is not a word one would apply, and, at this time of year, my days are usually filled with work and more work. My life, however, is rich, filled with gifts and the knowledge that my days are planned and ordered. This is not the first time I've told my Father, "It has been a good day," and I doubt it will be the last.

Life is good.

> This is the day that the LORD has made;
> let us rejoice and be glad in it.
> —Psalm 118:24

On Being Led

I never know with certainty where I am going to be or what I am going to be doing at any given point in time. I may make plans, but I always know those are subject to all kinds of variables beyond my control. When this day began, I had no idea I would end up in Jim's yard cleaning up debris.

It was quite rainy, and I had pretty much decided the day was going to be void of any outside work. By noon the four walls were closing in on me, so I headed out anyway, fully expecting to get soaked. The day did not turn out that way, though.

I believe most of us would like to live life with a sense of order, purpose, and direction. For as long as I can remember, this has been a personal desire of mine. A long time ago, the One who created me whispered, "I will lead you and guide you in the way you should go." At the time, I responded, "Yeah, whatever." As the years passed, I find I have gone back to that statement—that promise of life with order, purpose, and direction—over and over again, valuing it, claiming it as mine rather than giving it a casual, flippant response.

I *have* been led and guided—into life as a single person after thirty-seven years of marriage, into the job market when my only work experience on a résumé was several decades of being a stay-at-home mom to four children, into a gardening business where I am now able to mow and blow with the best of them, and into my own home. I could go on and on.

There are some who will say this way of living life is no different from living life on the fly, with a *whatever will be will be* mind-set. I adamantly maintain there is a vast difference. This is being grounded, connected to One who is larger than any person. Who knows me better than my Creator does? Who has higher goals and aspirations for me than I could ever imagine for myself? It's the parent-child scenario, where the parent wants only what is best for the child—except this is God the Father, and I am the child.

Which brings me back to Jim's yard. I never expected to go to Jim's today since he is a Tuesday client and today is Thursday. However, I was reminded of a pile of fallen branches in his yard. The rain cleared as I piled the debris in my truck. Jim will come home to a clean space, and I am able to cross off a project on my to-do list. As I worked, deep in thought, I once again felt grateful for being led and guided. Is this simplistic? Perhaps to some it could be, but for me it was powerful.

> I will instruct you and teach you the way you should go; I will counsel you with my eye upon you.
> —Psalm 32:8

On Life-Changing Events
Part 1: The Flood of 1964

life-changing: adj. Having a significant effect on the course of one's life.

Life is a very personal, individual matter, and life-changing events even more so. When such an event takes place, both the outer and the inner parts of one's life are affected—emotionally, mentally, spiritually. While making physical adjustments and compensations, an inner turmoil often follows. Settling into a place of peace, rest, and reconciliation may not take place for quite some time, if ever.

A bad-hair day does not constitute a life-changing event. Nor does the fact that, ever since I had some ignition work done on my truck, I hear a ding when I open the door whether or not the key is in the ignition. Those are annoyances, nuisances. A vacation when the weather will not cooperate or those three or four days that keep everyone housebound because of snow piled a foot deep does not qualify either.

Life-changing events are those times in our lives that create an emotional tornado or an earthquake that shake our very core. They are those times when everything is turned upside down. They mark a turning point in life, the events we use as *before* and *after* markers in our personal time line.

The Christmas flood of 1964 was that kind of an event for our young family. Several hundred miles away, a warm Chinook wind hit an early snowpack in the Cascade Mountains, melting it. That snowmelt ended up, literally, at our doorstep. The low-lying areas of the small coastal town where we lived filled with water, and that is where our home sat. Almost everything we owned was wiped out by an unusual set of circumstances. A young couple with a one-year-old son, we had moved into the area ten months earlier, relocating for a new job. We had no resources. The move and purchase of a mobile home had taken all the money we had. When the water subsided, we found ourselves homeless and broke.

Our lives had been completely altered, yet life continued on. I can still remember trying to set up a household after the flood in the small motel suite provided for us by the Red Cross. Our worldly possessions had been condensed into only those things that weren't affected by water. We were starting over from scratch. While the whole community was affected, I was dealing with my own private loss.

Many of you have probably experienced your own life-changing events and can relate. Perhaps it was a fire, a vehicle accident, a difficult medical diagnosis and prognosis, or a business failure. Life-changing events are varied and uniquely singular. And they are always personal.

We are given three choices whenever life hits us full on. We can turn *to* our Creator, we can turn *on* Him, or we can turn *away* from Him and deny the fact He even exists and cares. In my life I opt to seek Him and His help. Life is hard enough as it is. I prefer not doing it by myself when I don't have to.

I also believe that nothing is happenstance, that there is purpose and design to my life. Four months after that destruction, we found ourselves on two acres of country property, the site where we raised our four children and were able to give them "the best childhood any kid could ever have"—their quote, not mine.

The flood of 1964 was life-changing for me on many levels. Spiritual growth and maturity comes at a price sometimes. While often extremely difficult, it is invaluable. It is how growth takes place.

Part 2: The Rest of the Story

The flood of 1964 resulted in the loss of my family's home and almost everything in it. We were one of the fortunate ones covered by flood insurance. Since our mobile home had wheels, we were given the same kind of coverage as an automobile. While we did not receive a huge amount of money, it was at least something. Those who lived in regular houses were not afforded any protection or compensation at all.

Housing in the area was in short supply because an influx of population had come to work at a newly built paper mill, so we had no real options other than to replace the mobile home. Excitedly, we placed an order for our new home, unsure where we would set it up.

I refused to return to the mobile home park where we'd been flooded, so we had only one other setting in the small town that would accommodate our all-electric feature. We decided to place the trailer in the alternate park, even though it was a very crowded space. Having grown up in the country, being squeezed in on all sides didn't set well with me, but we had no other choice.

My husband worked the midnight shift at that time, also known as the graveyard shift. He was supposed to stop on his way home from work and place a deposit to hold our spot. Anxious to get home and get some sleep, he forgot three days in a row. Because we hadn't secured the site, it was given to someone else.

What should we do? A new mobile home would soon be delivered, and we had no place to put it. As we wrestled with the situation, my husband said, "Let's go find some property to put it on." In hindsight, this was quite a bold approach. We got in the car with our son and headed out with no direction in mind. We drove up a winding road we had never driven before, one which I was quite certain led nowhere. The road followed a creek, and two-and-one-half miles in we discovered a plot of land. I was proven wrong.

We had a whole one hundred dollars to our name, which we used as earnest money with the promise of nine hundred dollars for the down payment. It turned out we were able to claim our flood loss on taxes, and that nine hundred-dollar payment came just in time to finalize the deal. We had a place of our own to bring the mobile home to. Talk about timing!

Our home on Scholfield Road was a gift. I loved living there. The mobile home was replaced with a house as our family grew, and it became a gathering place for people of all ages. My children grew up there, and I would not trade that place or that time for anything.

Do you wonder why I live my life the way I do? The One who made me has taken such good care of me and continues to do so. He is the reason why.

> We know that all things work together for good for those who love God, who are called according to his purpose.
> —Romans 8:28

On Hospitality and a Thanksgiving Invitation

hospitality: n. The act or service of welcoming, receiving, hosting, or entertaining guests.

Thanksgiving is just around the corner. Perhaps that is the reason a certain memory floated through my mind today, an incident I hadn't thought about in years.

Pulp and paper mills operate twenty-four hours a day seven days a week, shutting down only periodically for repair and maintenance. As Thanksgiving Day 1966 approached, the prospects were dismal. Having moved a distance away from our hometown and from our families to be employed at the new mill, my husband was scheduled to work on the holiday.

There would be no extended-family dinner with a bounty of food and after-dinner traditions, no football games on television with the men in the family watching while the women crowded in the small kitchen, chatting and doing the dishes. There would be no chess game set up in the middle of the living room for my grandfather, uncle, and older brothers while the children created their own forms of entertainment. We would have to miss this annual family gathering.

Because we had just one car, I would be staying home alone with our three-year-old son. Living in the country, the neighbors were few and far between, amplifying the feeling of isolation and aloneness.

Holidays are often viewed as sacrosanct, exclusively reserved for card-carrying family members only. Some people would never consider inviting someone who isn't a relative. My own childhood has no memory of anyone other than family being included in holiday events, so when we received the invitation to a neighbor's Thanksgiving dinner, we hesitated to accept it.

A young woman herself, my neighbor's sincerity and warmth assured me we were welcome.

My husband, who worked rotating shifts, was scheduled to work day shift on Thanksgiving. He would come at the end of his workday, while my son and I went earlier. What a picture the two of us must have made as we trekked one-fourth mile down that winding country road on a chilly November day. My little boy had no idea where we were going or what we were going to do, but he was ever ready for an adventure.

I have no memory of the table setting, the meal, or who was present. I only remember being made to feel I had a place.

Hospitality isn't about being proper, about reciprocation, or even about being inclusive. It isn't about being the best hostess, the linens, the glassware, the dishes, or the elegant food. It is about being open and sharing oneself, and that is what I experienced.

I wonder if my hostess remembers that day. I have never forgotten it. I'm going to send a card this week, thanking her for her gracious hospitality and how much that Thanksgiving more than fifty years ago meant to me . . . and what it still means today.

This year's Thanksgiving will be spent at this same son's home. Though I doubt he has any memory of that one from his early childhood, and I've never even shared it with him, he, too, has an open-table policy where any and all who have no family or place to go are invited, included, and welcomed.

Kindness and hospitality go hand-in-hand, their effects impacting others far into the future.

> Do not neglect to show hospitality to strangers.
> —Hebrews 13:2

On Goals—Lofty, Realistic, and Others

goal: n. A result that one is attempting to achieve.

A vivid memory stands out in my mind. School had let out, and summer vacation was underway. I stopped to pick up some bread at the Sugar Shack, arguably the best bakery in the entire central Oregon coast area if not the world. While waiting to pay, someone asked if I had plans for the summer. I responded that my goal for the summer was to not cause bodily harm to my children and to return them safely to school in the fall. While exaggerated and certainly not the kindest of comments, there was an element of truth to it.

At that moment, I was serious. I was not the most patient mother in the world. Summer always brought its own set of complications, beginning and ending with several little girls and including the need to maintain a quiet environment for my husband, who often had to sleep during the day.

For whatever reason, my home was the gathering place for the children in the neighborhood. Throughout the summer, usually at least five little girls, including my own two, played in the yard, the woods, and the house. Sometimes cousins and additional friends came, adding even more. At times it wasn't too dissimilar from what is taking place between Israel and the Palestinians. All it took was one little girl to lob a verbal rocket into the group, and the peace was over. You get my drift.

Summer camps weren't an option, but Scholfield Road in the country was better than a camp as they spent hour upon hour clearing the forest floor, creating a house with rooms, and making paths, which they lined with rocks and swept clean with fallen conifer branches. There was plenty of room for them to roam, a small pond to explore, wild blackberries to pick, and snakes and critters to observe. Some wonderful memories were created, and once-in-a-lifetime adventures took place. However, my limited skills as camp counselor and peacemaker often pushed me to the max. Hence, the truth of my comment.

I pondered that memory as I worked one day. The bank of jasmine took a hard hit last winter and had a lot of dieback. The task of pruning the deadwood was monotonous and tedious but offered a wonderful time for contemplation and meditation. I found myself thinking about goals in general and a personal goal of mine.

Each of us has goals. Our aspirations and what we hope to achieve are individual and personal. I know of one who hopes to amass a specific dollar amount in this lifetime. Another expressed the goal of being a better person and father. Yet another wants to retire in another area of the country.

As for me, my goal is to stand before my Creator at the end of this physical life and have Him look me squarely in the eyes and state, "I do not regret having created you." "Regret?" you ask. "Surely, God has no regrets." As a gentle yet stark reminder, the destruction of the world by water during Noah's time was the result of God's regret when He looked upon humanity and saw the severity of wickedness prevalent in those He had created.

A great irony is that I am not a goal-oriented person. You'll not find me setting a goal for health, wealth, or self-improvement with the drive to complete it. That's not to say I haven't tried. It can be said I have not been successful. Experience has borne out the frustrations and failures of living that way, attempting to control my life and my destiny.

Some may say my goal is lofty and pious with an overlay of spiritual superiority. It carries none of those things. This is where my mind and my heart are. My goal can never be achieved by my efforts but only as God works in my life.

So perhaps I have not so much a goal but a heartfelt desire, one I hope is fulfilled.

> Set your minds on things that are above,
> not on things that are on earth.
> —Colossians 3:2

> For my thoughts are not your thoughts, nor
> are your ways my ways, says the Lord.
> —Isaiah 55:8

On Things That Make Me Go, "Hmm"

A friend is in the hospital, and I picked up a card to send to her. Recovery is going to take a while, so I wanted to get it in the mail in order to offer support. I had planned to put it in the mailbox before I went to work. Remembering I had left it in the truck, I went to retrieve it, but it was nowhere to be found. Having recently cleaned out the inside of my vehicle, I *knew* I had left it on the seat. I searched high and low, but it had essentially disappeared. I would have to stop by the store to purchase another card to accomplish the original goal.

A gentleman walked toward me as I approached the card section. Something about him seemed familiar. As I walked past, a name registered in my mind, but I said nothing. Heading off toward the checkout counter, I glanced down an adjacent aisle, saw him once again and decided to approach. "Excuse me. I think I know you," I said. Then I spoke his name and revealed mine. The name and the face were a match.

We had been neighbors up a little country road outside a small coastal town thirty years ago, and it had been that long since I'd seen him. We talked for quite a while alongside the shampoo section of the store—about that period of time, events of happiness and sadness since then, and our present circumstances. He now lives a short distance away—we are neighbors once again.

I paid for the card and headed for the truck. As soon as I opened the door, my eyes spotted the card, which I was certain had vaporized and disappeared. It wasn't even hidden from view, but I had repeatedly overlooked it in my search.

An unplanned trip to the store and a chance encounter brought one of those experiences that make me go, "Hmm." It wasn't an incident of epiphany, illumination, or discovery but one that left me with a sense of wonderment and an awareness of design and synchronization beyond any of my workings.

No one can figure out or understand these types of experiences. However, the way things line up and fall into place beyond my planning or control always fascinates and intrigues me.

At the base of all this is the fact that One greater than I is in charge of my life. This was just one of the things that make me go, "Hmm." Such experiences give me hope and an anchor in the midst of this crazy world exploding around us. God *is* in control.

On Close Encounters of the Small Kind

Rubbing my hand across my arm as I crawled out of bed, I began the day grateful that I had been stung only once. Most of my bicep was still swollen, red, and hot to the touch, but the itching had finally stopped at some point during the night. The day before, I had a close encounter of the small kind when I was stung by a little insect, a yellow jacket, which is a type of wasp.

The cycle of nature, including the gardening cycle, is running at least a month early this year. Winter came and went, barely making itself known. There is no snowpack in the mountains, the base that provides the water source for Oregon's reputation for lush vegetation. That lack has us all wondering what is going to happen as summer comes into full play. In addition, a lengthy, ferocious heat wave is quickly turning life brown.

My mind has been processing that thought for quite a while as I consider the habits of those tiny flying critters. A serious encounter with wasps two years ago when I dug into a ground nest has had me on edge at that time of the year ever since. Wasps become quite cranky as the end of summer nears, but everything this year is so early. I had my first wasp encounter of the season yesterday, and it's not even July yet.

We often say that catastrophic events are a big deal because they alter and affect our lives and our very existence. These include natural disasters, fire, life-threatening tragedies, health concerns, the loss of a job and income, stock market crashes, and calamitous accidents. However, I maintain that life can be just as markedly touched by what can only be viewed as a small thing.

Many years ago my family headed to a small airport so my son could catch a flight to return to school in Southern California after spending Christmas at home. The car, which was a boat of a station wagon, wasn't behaving well. After saying our goodbyes at the airport, we decided to head back to my parents' house forty-five minutes away rather than continue the trip home, which was a much longer drive.

The sky had been spitting snow as we left the airport, and the farther we traveled the more inclement the weather became. So too, the farther we traveled, the more sluggish the car. Darkness fell as we crawled along at a snail's pace on a side road rather than the freeway. It became obvious that wisdom was keeping people in their homes instead of venturing out since there was no traffic. Blizzard-like conditions prevailed, with snow blowing sideways and visibility at a bare minimum.

After traveling just a few miles, the car came to a halt beside a small cemetery out in the middle of farmland. Three children and two adults were stranded on a country road in the midst of what turned out to be a wicked blizzard, one that gnarled traffic and brought the valley floor to a halt for two weeks before the ice and snow melted.

In a time before cell phones, we had no plan. We were caught by surprise. We had no blankets in the car and no flashlights. It was dark and cold, and growing colder and bleaker by the minute. The lights of a house shone barely visible in the distance. My husband decided to walk there for help. Just then a truck with a horse trailer drove past, coming from the opposite direction. We assumed they had just driven on by, but, instead, they went down the road to find a place to turn around so they could come back to help.

And help they did. They transported us to their warm home, fed us leftovers from Christmas dinner, and housed us for the night until a family member could pick us up the next day.

Our car was taken to a local mechanic for repair. It turned out a fly had gotten into the carburetor, making it a "flyberator," as described by one of my daughters. My knowledge of automobile mechanics is minimal at best, but from what I understand it is impossible for a fly to get into a carburetor. And yet there it was.

Our lives were altered by one little fly, with the potential of serious ramifications.

There is a point and purpose to all things. I am of the belief that the chance timing of a disabled vehicle on the road in a snowstorm and the kind generosity of strangers was the result of the care and provision of my heavenly Father. I would suspect three girls, who are now grown women, feel the same. I know the adults do.

Today I drove by the place where we were stranded almost thirty-five years ago. I always remember what happened, and I am always grateful. I never take that experience for granted.

May your experiences in life be seen with a new perspective and with spiritual lenses, not just natural ones. It isn't the big things in life but also the small ones that are given to us so we might learn, grow, and experience God in our everyday lives.

On the Christmas Spirit

spirit: n. The manner or style of something.

It's that time of the year—Christmastime. There is enough sugar and fat in the excessive amounts of candy, cookies, and goodies being produced in kitchens everywhere to clog the arteries of the strongest of men. Christmas baking for me consists of melting chocolate chips in the microwave and adding a variety of ingredients to create delectable treats. If not enough to cause a heart attack, they have the potential to at least make a person very sick.

As a gardener, I dispose of grass clippings, weeds, and branches at a local business. The debris is shredded and converted to compost or other planting mediums. I maintain it's the perfect enterprise. They charge me for my dumping. Then I pay for a completed product, one for which I have provided the basic resource.

The dump site is managed by several young men, most in their twenties. As tends to happen while I am out and about, I have become acquainted with some of them as they share parts of their lives while I am paying to dump my load. I know that one of them was recently married. Another is taking some time off from college in order to get a better perspective on the direction he wants to go. Another played football in high school and now spends his weekends in a royal battle of sorts. They greet me with a smile and know by now I will refuse their offer to help me unload.

I purchased a large container and will fill it to the brim with candy. Then I'll drop it off at the refuse site today for them to share. One could say I have the Christmas spirit.

Being filled with the Christmas spirit is not a phrase typically applied to me. The holiday itself is simply not that important to me. Lights, decorating, the tree—these are all things I can live without. A daughter expressed it well when she said, "You always did and have put on a good Christmas face for your kids and grandkids." It's good to know I haven't mortally damaged my family's love for the holiday.

Although it seems a contradiction, I make ornaments for each of the children and grandchildren every year, add my share to the gifts under the tree, and have established a tradition of selfless gift-giving for the grandgirls by providing them money to donate to others. I do not have a love for this holiday. But I have no love for any other holiday either.

Holidays come, and holidays go. And so it will be with Christmas.

Over the years I have wrestled with what could only be perceived as a negative outlook regarding the holiday. I questioned the point of bringing a tree into the house and the obscene amount of stuff collected under that tree, all culminating in said gifts being dispersed, many to be forgotten before the next holiday comes along.

This is where I have landed, however: One day out of 365 is not a statement of a person's life. Kindness, generosity, empathy, caring, selflessness, and love are important qualities that need to be manifest in one's daily life and not limited to presenting a beautifully wrapped package to be opened on Christmas. They are traits that should be applied to all parts of life, not just during a particular season.

And so in a personal gesture, also known as "having the Christmas spirit," I head out with my very large container of candy, delivering it to the guys at Rexius Fuel. It is my way of thanking them for revealing parts of their lives to me and for allowing me to get to know them. People matter—holidays, not so much.

On a Covered Bridge Picture

The beauty of the covered bridge caused me to stop the truck, get out, and take a picture. I was heading home after spending the day cleaning a vacation home for a client. The trip up the McKenzie River that morning provided an exceptional feast for the eyes and the soul. I had not driven that road for several years, and I relished the entire excursion. I looked forward to the repeated scenery on my way back.

It had taken around an hour to get to my destination, and I expected it to be the same on the return trip. I texted my daughters and gave them an estimated time of arrival. About twenty minutes into the drive, traffic ground to a halt. As sirens sounded in the distance and an ambulance and police cars arrived, it was evident an accident had occurred ahead. The seriousness of the situation became clear as drivers turned off their engines, left their cars, and walked to get a better view. There was no doubt traffic would be stopped for a while.

Information began trickling back. Two men returning from the scene reported that a car with a mother and her two children had crashed. One of the children was in critical condition, the other still trapped inside the car and the mother's fate unknown. She had been coming from the opposite direction and, for whatever reason, had veered across the westbound lane and collided with the rock wall.

I informed my daughters of the delay via another text, and the waiting continued. After almost an hour, the highway opened to one lane of traffic. It was then I realized this accident had happened right ahead of me, one-fourth mile at most, just around the curve. There were no more than eight cars between my vehicle and the crash. Driving past the mangled chunk of metal, which now barely resembled a car, I was sobered. Lives were forever changed in a split second.

I drove home in that frame of mind, the beauty along the

McKenzie River never registering. I remembered stopping to take the picture of the covered bridge. It took less than a minute. If I had not stopped, my truck and I would probably have been in proximity of that careening vehicle. Do I know that for an absolute fact? It isn't so much an argument of fact as it is a sense, an awareness.

Why is one spared and another isn't? Why am I able to say a covered bridge picture may have been what saved me from a terrible accident, yet another family is experiencing suffering and pain at this very moment? I have no easy answer. My daughter expressed it well when she said, "I'm thankful too (for you) and feel horrible for the family that is dealing with it."

We all experience hard times, and, without making light of those times or being facetious or trite, there is absolutely nothing easy about them. The very use of the word *accident*, with its connotation of chance, is a misnomer.

It is my belief that nothing is random, coincidental, or happenstance, and that there is a point and purpose to all things. Are they always painless, simple, uncomplicated? No. Do they always make sense, and do we have understanding? No. And, most often, not at all in the beginning, in the initial phases of those experiences. Are they part of a greater plan? Yes.

The lives of a mother, her two children, and their family and friends have been forever changed by a drive along the McKenzie River. For me, it serves as a stark reminder that my life is not my own, and that God alone is in control.

> For from him and through him and to him are all
> things. To him be the glory forever. Amen.
> —Romans 11:36

On Being OK

OK: adj. In good health or a good emotional state.

Upon greeting me, a friend often asks, "How are you, Ladonna?"

"I'm OK," I typically respond.

"Just OK?" he questions.

I usually laugh and answer, "It's better than not OK."

Heading out to mow, it was four weeks to the day since I took an inglorious spill in a crosswalk in downtown Boise, Idaho. There was nothing casual about the fall, no trip and stumble, but rather a splat to the street.

A visit to the emergency room verified my initial comment as I pulled myself up: "My jaw is jacked up." An X-ray confirmed that it was indeed. I had actually broken my jaw.

There is no cast for a broken jaw, and, in order for it to be stabilized, extreme braces were put in place. The initial plan was for screws to be placed in the gums and then wires attached. The correct wire wasn't available, so plan B included braces with bands. Thank God.

"Liquids only for six weeks," I was told. At first, I could ingest liquids from a syringe through a very small tube. After twelve days I would be promoted to just the syringe. No chewing allowed. My blender became my best friend.

Adjustments were made as I filled the fridge with protein- and calorie-rich dairy products and shakes, maximizing meals with as many legumes as possible, creating dishes with combinations of a variety of foods to provide the eighty grams of daily protein suggested by a dietitian. I was never able to come close to that.

Settling into the process of physical healing, I wasn't prepared for the need to be healed emotionally.

My family insisted I stay with them for the first several days, despite my claim that I was fine. Surrounding me with love and protection, it was the perfect environment and cocoon in which to begin healing. In retrospect, I wasn't as fine as I thought I was.

Pain was never an issue. Having the rug pulled out from underneath me was.

The lack of confidence and the sense of being unsure of myself and of basic motor movements came like a wave hitting the rocks, unannounced at random moments. I found the fall had shaken me.

The first time I went to the grocery store alone, I sat in the truck, steeling myself. My family had supported me for ten days, and now I was on my own. Cautiously, gauging every step and every flaw in the pavement, I headed out. Knowing my inability to talk and be understood because of the restrictive banding, my instinct was to retreat, but an empty larder and the need to feed myself won out.

Fear has its residence in the unknown, and all life is just that—unknown. The "what ifs" took over. What if I fall again? What if the jaw isn't fully healed and I damage it yet again? What if? What if?

I had to force myself to cross the street to get my mail from the mailbox. Holing up inside my house, curling into a ball, and staying there almost seemed easier and quite inviting.

A client who has had several bad falls with serious injuries described them as being traumatic—a new concept to consider. That description matched some of what I had been feeling, including a real sense of vulnerability.

Going back to work was my version (or make that God's version) of being pushed out of the nest. I fought it, yet at the same time, I knew it was important for my well-being. I needed to get back in a familiar routine again. I did only cleaning that first week. I tested any unexpected ramifications from using the vacuum cleaner, leaning over while working, or anything that might cause a shift in the jaw area.

I mowed for the first time almost a month after falling. It was the first time since my fall that I had off-loaded and loaded the mower from the truck, the first time I had started my tools by pulling on the rope starter. Did this put too much pressure on the healing jaw? Was my ear protection pressing against it? So much of the body is used in the simplest of motions. Was I causing unseen damage?

Peace was not my friend as I concluded my day and headed home. Pulling into the garage and turning the engine off, I heard my inner voice say, *I am not OK. I am not OK. I am not OK.* Over and over again, it spilled out until I was emptied. Only silence remained as I headed inside. Then, very quietly, I heard, "You are OK."

So many times we want to be great, fantastic, fabulous, outstanding, and superb. But those are often bubbles that quickly burst and disappear. My position is that being "just OK" is a good thing.

And I am OK.

> Peace I leave with you; my peace I give to you. I do not give to you as the world gives. Do not let your hearts be troubled, and do not let them be afraid.
> —John 14:27

On Regret

regret: n. Emotional pain on account of something done or experienced in the past with a wish that it had been different; a looking back with dissatisfaction or with longing.

"So, Ladonna, what is your story?" he asked. I found I was at a loss for words, which was extremely rare for me.

The young man and I had recently been introduced to each other. This was his way of becoming better acquainted while we worked together in a client's garden.

The question was one I had never been asked before. A deluge of thoughts instantly filled my mind like water released through floodgates. How does one condense a span of seventy-one years into a few sentences?

I ended up telling him where I was born and raised. I shared that I grew up on a farm, where my father fed our family from a huge garden and large orchard, with my mother freezing and preserving it all. I said that we had a small herd of milk cows and raised the beef our family ate. I explained that my childhood was simple yet rich, though not in a monetary sense. These were basic facts about my life, but I realized that was not *my story*.

Each of us has a story. Our stories are uniquely individual, and we are the sole possessors of them. There are no duplicates.

One of my clients passed away several months ago, but I continue maintaining the garden since the property has been placed on the market for sale. The lawn needed mowing today, and as I was edging it, I heard myself tell my Father, "Thank You for my life. I have no regrets."

Regret is an insidious cohort. Time is always moving forward. Reliving the past or starting over is not an option. The *what-ifs* and *if-only*s can grow within one's mind, gradually taking over and becoming obsessions until we are unable to live in the present.

The piano has been a part of my life for as long as I can remember. I began taking lessons when I was five. As a young girl of perhaps nine or so, I was offered the opportunity to study at Juilliard via a correspondence course facilitated by my piano teacher. My parents declined. I don't know their reasoning. I was neither consulted nor involved in the decision. In fact, we never spoke of the opportunity or the decision.

I didn't give the incident much thought until years later. It was then I got caught up in an imaginary world. What if I had gone down that road? Would I be a world-famous concert pianist now? What had I missed out on? What had my parents denied me? My mind was consumed.

As time passed, I realized I had been given a gift. Life as a classical pianist would not have suited me. It would have been a perfect setting for a self-centered, self-involved attitude to thrive and explode. I would have been of no earthly good to anyone, absorbed by and focused on one thing and one thing only—myself.

As a pianist being schooled in classical music, the quest for perfection had already begun to diminish the pure joy of playing and making music. In that world there would have been very little gratification, living with comparisons to others and the judgments of never being quite good enough, always striving for an elusive gold star. In addition, the competition in the music world is fierce, and I probably would not have even survived the cut of the very elite—the equivalent of failure.

The hypothetical speculation about a road not taken was replaced with the realization that I have no regrets.

At the end of high school, I made the decision to get married instead of attending college. It wasn't based on finances as there probably would have been resources available. The reason was very personal, one that many felt defied logic.

As I am wont to do, when I make such a decision I don't look back, and I didn't.

The base of all things and all life is spiritual. Instead of training as a classical pianist or preparing for a career in a variety of fields, I was given another kind of education, one specifically designed for me at the feet of God. My story is founded on that walk, getting to know Him as a person, learning how to live with Him, and being stretched beyond the physical into the spiritual.

Fast-forward almost fifty-four years, and I find I am a self-employed gardener who mows lawns, weeds gardens, prunes shrubs, and grubs around in the dirt. I have no other career, have no degree beyond high school, and have none of the perks that go along with those things, such as financial stability and resources.

The desire of my life since I was young has been to make a difference for all eternity. I have only one life, and I have been taught how to live it well. I am a wealthy woman, for I have that which money cannot buy.

I suggest you examine your life, your story, before our Father. And may you also have no regrets in this life or the one to come.

It Takes Two: On Being an Instrument

instrument: n. A device used to produce music; a means or agency for achieving an effect.

If you were to ask me to describe the instrument, I would do so in the most elementary of terms. If the same request was applied to the music that comes from it, I would have to search for adequate words. How does one explain the experience of being captivated and enraptured by a musician and his instrument? It transcends all adjectives and vocabulary.

"You have one more chance," my client said. I had come to blow debris off his driveway with my blower, and he referred to my refusal several weeks earlier of a ticket to the symphony. Bone-tired, I had begged off then and asked for a rain check. And here it was. "Would you like a ticket to hear Yo-Yo Ma play?" he asked. My jaw dropped. I was not going to refuse this invitation. I resolved to get a good night's rest before heading off to the concert.

The cello is a large instrument in the violin family. Made of wood, it has four strings that are played with a bow. The end pin rod holds the cello planted in the floor while it's played.

From my vantage point in the audience, this instrument of the world-renowned virtuoso looked very similar to those of his fellow cellists in the orchestra. It may or may not have been his Venetian cello, crafted in 1733 by Antoni Stradivari. Known as the Montagnana, that cello is valued at $2.5 million. But, then again, Yo-Yo Ma looked as ordinary as his fellow musicians in the orchestra as well.

That changed when he began to play. It wasn't just the music that flowed from the cello, but also the experience of watching as man and instrument became one. I found myself holding my breath as he pulled his bow back and forth across the strings on the final note of the song, the sound floating off into the air. The audience was mesmerized. We sat completely silent before bursting into thunderous applause.

A child prodigy, Yo-Yo Ma had been challenged by one of his teachers in his early years to "pull the soul of the composition through the strings" of the cello. He performed with the desire to "make the music live" and to "hear that special hush." And he certainly does. "The instrument is my voice," he says.

I found myself considering the instrument and its spiritual application.

There is a gross misunderstanding and false perception in the world *and* in the religious realm when it comes to God and the manner in which He works with people, bringing about His will and revealing Himself on this earth. Those who speak in spiritual terms often use catchphrases. They say they are "being used by God" or they are "His tool, His instrument." This suggests that He is a puppet master and we are the puppets being controlled. It is a natural response to resist and turn away from this image of God.

"Bless the fruits of our labors" was a common prayer heard during my childhood. While an honorable idea, prayers such as these may carry the implication that we are able to bring about change through our own efforts. These suggest we are able to do something to make the world a better place if God would just help us. Many prayers invoke His blessing on those good deeds.

The reality is that living life with God is a collaboration as He and I work together. Living life with Him isn't my working for Him or being *used* by Him, but rather staying in tune *with* Him. Yes, I am His instrument, and it takes the two of us.

The Montagnana was created for the purpose of producing beautiful music, but this can happen only at the hand of a master. Yo-Yo Ma was given the gift of making music, but that can happen only if he has an instrument. It takes two.

The cello's purpose is fulfilled simply by being, not by doing. Do you see it?

And so it is with God and us. Being His instrument is in the *being,* not the doing. And that is when beautiful music is made—from Him and at His hand.

> I am the vine, you are the branches. Those who
> abide in me and I in them bear much fruit, because
> apart from me you can do nothing.
> —John 15:5

Chapter 5

Aging, Death, and Eternity

For the Love of Dog

His name is Tank, the name given to him fourteen years ago when he was chosen as a puppy. Barrel-chested and the largest of the litter, wherever he went he readily made his way with the ease of a military armored vehicle. It was as apropos then as it is now. In his prime he weighed 110 pounds. As an elder, that has diminished to eighty-nine pounds, but he's still a large animal.

Tank's family went on a camping trip. In times past he would have been included. With age have come some physical restrictions. The logistics of navigating the campsite and trailer would be difficult for him and not practical, so he has come to stay at my house.

He loves going into the backyard, investigating the trails of animals that may have frequented it during the night, and lying on the cool grass.

There are two steps from the utility room to outside. Tank's hips are weakening, and he has trouble hoisting his massive body up onto his back legs. Very carefully, he gauges placement of his paws as he works his way down, which is no small feat for an animal his size.

Coming back in is no easy matter either as demands are placed on his front legs and upper body to get up the steps and through the door, but his back legs are unable to provide the necessary spring sometimes. I leave the back door open for him, and he comes up to the steps and stands, waiting for me to coax and encourage him. He senses his limitations, and when the legs simply aren't working, he waits as I get a blanket and place it beneath his back hip area. With willingness and effort, he works with me as I raise his front half in the door, supporting the lower portion of his body with the sling. With some of the weight relieved, he is then able to get his back legs underneath him and step up and in.

For the first two years of his life, he had the exclusive attention of his owner and master; they were the picture of "a man and his dog." With love and a firm hand, Tank was taught the importance of manners and obedience.

The family grew. A wife, an infant, and then another one entered the household, and Tank was unsure of his status. He had lost the position of first priority, and it was evident he didn't understand what was happening. Jealousy is not in his nature, and he conceded to the change. With his body size and bulk, there was the potential of plowing the little ones over, but he was always conscious of them and did his best to make way for them. Now ages ten and twelve, the girls claim "Tankers" as their best friend.

Observing the process of aging can be troublesome, whether it be man or beast. Tank's abilities and capabilities have decreased since the last time he stayed with me. His body is wearing out. The days of chasing after a ball, swimming in the river, and running forever have passed.

Tank is aging gracefully. His intelligence and level of awareness regarding his physical state is amazing, his disposition and spirit admirable. The dignity with which he is living his life at this stage is remarkable. He copes with his restrictions and does so with a smile. It's an example his human friends could readily follow.

Do animals have a place in the next life? Tank has caused me to give that some serious thought. While I have no definitive or conclusive answer, I do know the Creator cares about all His creation, and that includes Tank.

Without words, Tank has had an impact on many. A gift to his family and those who come in contact with him, he certainly has worked his way into my heart. Lessons learned from an animal at the hand of God.

On Aging

aging: v. The process of becoming older or more mature.

Several days ago, my daughter sent me a picture of the two of us, one I had not seen before. I asked her when it was taken and who the old lady was who was with her. There was an apparent conflict, a two- to three-decade disparity between what I saw with my eyes and how I felt. I don't feel old; however, pictures don't lie, and this one did not.

It was the summer of my sixty-ninth year when my body began to betray me. This refrain has been floating through my mind for days now, weeks even. It sounds like it should be the opening sentence of a book or even the beginning line of a song, doesn't it? It is both of these. It is the story of my present life and the words of a song permeating my being.

My father was a muscular beast of a man. His stature wasn't overly large, but he was a picture of strength and sinewy muscle. He cut his eye teeth on hard physical labor. As a young man, he and his brother sold firewood they cut by hand with a crosscut saw. I remember watching him when I was a little girl as he wielded gunnysacks filled with grain and manhandled countless bales of hay. To say the farming kept him active and strong is an obvious understatement.

A vivid memory of him stands out in my mind. As an older man, probably in his seventies, he was dressed in his Sunday best. As he showed me his upper arm, he referenced my grandfather. "I remember when Granddad told me he'd lost his muscle tone," Dad said. The same thing had happened to Dad. I'm not sure if he was preparing me or just sharing. Probably both.

And now here I am at sixty-nine. The gardening business keeps me active. I haul equipment in and out of my truck every day, carry bags filled with debris, and dispose of them as well. On occasion, I have flexed my bicep to verify the physical labor involved. However, a change is taking place in my body. As with my father and my grandfather, the muscle tone is diminishing. *Buff* is not a word applied to those in my age group. We may be described as strong or active or in good shape—with the qualifier "for his/her age"—but very rarely are we described as buff.

Much of my gardening clientele are around my age. Aging and change are often part of our discussions. One client recounted the body parts bothering her—shoulder, hands, feet, back. Another peer categorizes all the physical changes and maladies as OA, meaning old age. A common topic of conversation amongst older folk, aging is a reality of everyday life.

As this theme song continued wafting through my brain, I began thinking about the fact that aging is a process as are many things related to the body. There is the birthing process, the healing process, the maturing process, and the dying process. The very word itself is indicative of something taking place over a period of time. It does not happen overnight, but it does happen.

I have always been fascinated by life's cycles and how our lives often go full circle. We end up where we began. We started this life being taken care of. We were fed, clothed, bathed. Our basic needs were provided for. If not for the care given, we all would have perished. At that time we never had a concern over bills, budgets, the weather, groceries, schedules, appointments—a way of life not all that different from the assisted care provided to an older person.

We eagerly awaited the magical age when we could obtain a driver's license, a rite of passage providing independence. At the other end of the spectrum, the license isn't renewed, the keys to the car are taken away, and driving privileges are revoked because of age-related issues. Perhaps we suffer from slow reaction times, vision problems, or confusion. A life of independence shifts into a life of dependency.

Flexibility, agility, strength, balance, and coordination are mastered by infants, but they are also the very abilities and qualities that become fragile upon aging. The circle of limitations and boundaries that began in infancy often ends as the conclusion of life is approached.

Reality is always another story, and at sixty-nine I'm not sure I still view these cycles as fascinating.

The body does betray us as we age. Those elements we once relied on and even took for granted are no longer present. The aging process is part of life. It is not personal; it is universal. I guess I just expected it to circumvent me.

This much I know: Having a sense of humor and a positive attitude at any point in life is priceless. Having a daughter who says, "You're gorgeous," when you know the two of you are looking at the same picture is even more so. While progress can't be stopped, neither can the aging process. I am grateful one can look old and be old yet not *feel* old.

On Learning What It Means to Trust

trust: v. To place confidence in; to rely on, to confide, or have faith in.

My mother would have called me a worrywart, and she would have been accurate. The cold, hard facts are that I have been in a state of worry for a while. In fact, if I had a worry stone, one of those rocks that is supposed to provide relief from stress or anxiety by rubbing it, I would have rubbed it so hard its size would have diminished right before my eyes.

My seventieth birthday is on its way. I call it my seventieth gig. Its approach has caused a whole list of issues to surface as my mind finds itself in a completely different place than it has been with any previous birthday. My peers will either already know or understand. The rest of you will figure it out in due time.

The issues are not contrived, and they deserve consideration. How much longer am I going to be able to work as a gardener? Am I going to survive financially? What health issues are awaiting me? What is going to happen to me as I continue aging? How many more years are left for me on this earth? How many more years will I share in the lives of my grandgirls? While the concerns are valid, worry is not productive but counterproductive.

One of the things I like about my Creator is that He is not like a super hero. He doesn't come into my life to save the day. What He *does* do is allow me to *be* me as I process thoughts, go in circles, and spin around into oblivion in that worry state. When I've worn myself out, He may interject a thought and reveal a step or a direction. Even then it is my choice to consider it or to continue like a ball bouncing around in a pinball machine.

The thought was subtle, but I could not deny hearing it. *Do you trust Me?* Now I know better than to try to pull the wool over

God's eyes by glibly responding. He knows me better than I know myself, and there are no right or wrong answers, only honest ones. So I thought . . . and thought . . . and thought some more. I could not even come up with a definition of what that word meant. There was a general concept, but it was absolutely nothing I could put into words. I responded, "I don't know, but I would like to."

After a trip to the dictionary, I still had no real understanding of the meaning of trust. It was just a word, similar to viewing a one-dimensional picture with no depth.

There were gentle reminders of experiences in my life, three of them in one day, and my own offhanded comment that "I am being taken care of." God was building the case that He was worthy of being trusted.

Several thoughts began forming within me. One was the knowledge that where there is worry, there is no peace. Peace and worry cannot coexist. Another is that I have no control over anything in my life. Circumstances can change in an instant, and there is nothing I can do to alter them. My life and its future are out of my hands. And then there is the fact that to not believe God is the same as calling Him a liar. That word *trust* began to take form and gain dimension and shape.

As I began understanding what it means to trust, I realized trust had begun to develop within me. I did not expect that or know it was going to happen, but it has. Some may question why I would want to place my trust in One who is unseen; others may find it absurd since they doubt the very existence of God. For me, He is part of my life and the way I live my life.

It is the nature of humans to be self-sufficient and independent. "No, thank you. I can do it myself," is a common response. People do not readily turn over control of their lives to someone else or place unwavering trust in another. However, the bottom line of it all is I am either going to trust myself or trust the One who made me.

So what does it mean to trust my Father? It means I rely on Him to take care of me, to watch out for me, to be beside me each and every step of my life. It means *knowing* these things.

I cannot say I am there yet, fully living in a level of trust, but I am in a better place than I have been in recent days as I learn what it means to trust. And I hope the next time He asks, "Do you trust Me?" I will be able to say, "Yes!"

> O Lord my God, in thee do I put my trust.
> —Psalm 7:1 (kjv)

On the Things I Have Learned in the Process of Turning Seventy

process: n. A series of events to produce a result, not a product.

Life and the living of it is a process. Beginning as a single cell, conception takes place. That cell divides, and the process continues. With all life, be it human or animal, there are specific, precise steps that take place within the womb until the time when physical development has reached the point where life can survive outside the maternal incubator provided. And the process continues as life goes on.

There was a time when I wanted life to be instantaneous—answers given, problems solved, issues resolved, situations set right with a snap of the fingers. I had no grasp of either the concept or the importance of process.

Not all that long ago, a dramatic turn of events took place in my life. A wise friend told me, "Healing takes time. It is a process." I nodded in agreement, pretending I understood. I didn't. The need for healing and its process was beyond my comprehension. It took some time; however, I see it now, and I greatly appreciate this thing called *process*.

And so it has been with my turning seventy—a process. Many of my peers, especially those from my school days, are a bit older than I. My parents had me begin grade school at age five, so I was always the youngest in my class. Because of that, I am reaching the seventieth plateau later than many I grew up with.

This particular birthday has been on its way for—well, for at least a year. I watched and observed as friends and family wrestled with the big 7-0. I even gave advice and expressed some valid truths. But, as with all things, I had no understanding of the experience until it was my turn. Experience *is* the best teacher.

One's tenth birthday is exciting, having finally reached double digits. The importance in that is elusive, depending upon the one turning ten. At the age of twenty, youth is one's friend and a level of independence has been reached. The future is at hand. When thirty arrives, some goals and aspirations may have been achieved, and that may include sharing life with a spouse and children. Forty comes quickly after, as time seems to pass at an accelerated rate of speed, and with it comes an urgency to become accomplished, whether in a personal sense or a professional one. When fifty appears on the scene, the reality of having lived half a century begins to settle in. It's as though one is on a fulcrum, and the balance begins to shift as one heads down the other side. Then there is sixty. For many, that decade means retirement and the reference "senior citizen" becomes applicable.

Turning seventy is readily viewed by many as a milestone for a variety of reasons. The most common is the reality of the brevity of time left on this earth. The starkness of that can be difficult and crippling.

I believe this birthday can either make or break a person. The same process that took place while in the embryotic state is still in play, a continuation of life, except there is evidence and personal experience of the aging of the body.

And this is where I feel there is the potential for breaking a person. In the process of approaching seventy, I found myself in that mental place, stuck in a revolving door as I began viewing myself as *being* old. Everything in my life was correlated to my age, including every physical and mental stumble. None of it was positive, but a virtual breeding ground for fear. Viewing life from the platform of being seventy is completely different from that of a younger person, and the potential is in place for a grim outlook.

While in that negative mode, stuck in the revolving door within my mind, a friend said bluntly, "Get over it. Move on." He spoke of "making peace with turning seventy," which is one of the best pieces of advice anyone gave me. And in doing that, I was booted out the door to the other side.

In addition to learning that turning seventy can be a mental booby trap, I learned it really is just a number, an indicator of the total years I have physically inhabited this earth and this body. It does not define me. It does not say anything about the kind of person I am or what I feel or think. No number is an identification of any person regardless the age. Rather it is a simple description, no different from eye color, hair color, height, or weight.

I've asked people of various ages how old they feel on the inside in comparison to their chronological age. To a person, the response is easily several decades younger. I am not the same person I was in my twenties—thank God!—or my forties, or even a week ago. While my body is indeed aging, my soul and spirit are growing and developing, and that is what I revel in.

Life is a process, and in that process I had a seventieth birthday. Arriving at that day did not happen in a day or a week. It took time, but when that day came, I was prepared for it. I am grateful for the process that led me there, the steps that made it possible for me not to be stuck on the dark side of that event, living in fear. I am thankful for those my Father used along the way as well as for their understanding and their ears.

It is my position that, from the time of conception, my heavenly Father is a Master at designing, choreographing, and implementing various processes in the lives of His children. I made it to seventy, and I am already on the other side—with a smile on my face.

And life moves on. Will I make it to eighty? That is probably another story for another day a few years down the road.

On Living with Mortality

mortality: n. The condition of being susceptible to death.

immortality: n. The condition of not being susceptible to death.

Across the board without exception—regardless of age, station in life, gender, or where we live on the planet—this is something we all do. As part of this human race, each of us lives with mortality, whether or not it is acknowledged, denied, accepted, or even realized.

It has been said the only two things we can be sure of in this life are death and taxes. From the time of conception, we live under that known reality, a death sentence of the physical body. The one unknown is the timing of it, whether it will come sooner or later.

Arguments are made for and against various causes, issues, and points of view. People disagree on almost everything—religious, political, or social—but there is no disagreement on the status of human mortality. It is never challenged or argued. It cannot be. Mortality is a universal equalizer.

A family member in his late eighties passed away, and a mental picture came to mind. It was of the sea with the tide rolling in. As the waves worked their way in and then receded, the beach was swept clean. "Look around," I heard. "How many people do you see who are 125 years old?" One picture is worth a thousand words. There is not one who will not be taken from this physical life.

So how does one live with mortality without negativity? How does one live without being overcome by depression or viewing life through lenses of morbidity?

Some create a bucket list, with the intent to live life to its fullest, doing as much as humanly possible and fulfilling wishes and desires. For others, a deep resignation takes place as fear of the unknown lurks, hidden in the shadows. Still others develop an attitude of denial and decide, *I'm just not going to think about it.* On a personal level, my sense of mortality is countered by my belief in immortality.

When I was very young, my grandmother told me of her near-death experience. She had been seriously ill with a severe fever—perhaps rheumatic fever—and it wasn't certain if she was going to survive. When she finally began to recover, she told of being in an unspoiled place with green fields everywhere and a warm light. She knew it was life after death.

It is my belief—no, I have the knowledge and conviction—that the end of my physical life is only the beginning of another way of life, one governed by eternity, and I am but a breath away from entering into that realm. I have no fear of death. If possible, when it happens I would like to be the one who returns to tell you about everything that awaits you. But then my experiences will never make a believer out of others. You have to have your own.

> When this perishable body puts on imperishability, and this mortal body puts on immortality, then the saying that is written will be fulfilled: "Death has been swallowed up in victory."
> —1 Corinthians 15:54

On Death

death: n. Cessation of life and all associated processes.

No longer with us, passed over, passed away, moved on to a better place, free at last—a variety of terms are used to express death, many of them meant to soften the harshness of that reality.

There has been a death in our family. Our stepmother died. At the age of ninety-eight, she was the last of our parents' generation. The torch has been passed on to my two brothers and me. We are now the elders of the Shanks family.

Death fascinates and intrigues me. In fact, I think about it often. It is universal, a common denominator. Not a single person on the planet is exempt from its sentence. Where there is life, there will be death.

How is it that the essence of a person can be removed after one breath, one heartbeat, leaving only the empty house, the body? What happens when this physical body gives out?

Death is not something to be feared. We have been created as eternal beings in the image of our Creator. Given that, this life is just the beginning, with eternal life continuing on after our physical death.

My mother suffered from Alzheimer's for ten years. Communication was limited at best. She did, however, experience rare moments of clear lucidity before the confusion took over again. During one visit, she looked at me and said, "I was walking down a road and came up to a door. The door opened, and there He stood . . . just as big as life."

"Who?" I asked.

"Well, God. Who do you think?"

"Were you afraid of Him?"

"Well, no. Should I have been?" And then she spoke no more.

Death is quite simply a transition into the next stage of life, where life is lived in a different way, in a different place. In a sense, that next stage is no different from our physical life. We will either continue living with God or without Him. And it is as simple as walking through a door.

My family and I will gather at a funeral service. At these occasions I can't help but think, *Who's next?* Only God knows.

This I do know: We enter this world alone, and we leave it alone. We will take nothing of this earth with us when we die. Given the universal experience of death, what is truly important is that of being prepared to meet God. May He help each of you with this. Preparation for the next life is a very good thing.

It is appointed for mortals to die once, and after that the judgment.
—Hebrews 9:27

On Being Prepared

preparation: n. The act of preparing or getting ready.

Whenever I hear of or think of those who have passed away, I find myself wondering, *Where are they now? What are they doing? What did they find in the next life?* Some may consider that unnatural, grim, or even macabre. I find it realistic. Life does not end when a final breath is taken on this earth but continues on in another realm, one that is spiritual yet actual. This life is temporal and short-term. The next is eternal.

The afterlife, as it is often called, is conjured up in the mind to be almost like a fairy tale, as if the life left on earth just continues. The possibility and probability of it being as people imagine is certainly remote. Our imaginings are natural, a human response to deal with ideas and concepts that are larger than life. After all, how can we begin to conceive of that which we've never seen? And it's not like a tourist site, a cruise ship, or hotel accommodations, where friends go and then return with their critiques and recommendations or the lack thereof.

People spend an inordinate amount of time planning and preparing for situations and circumstances in life—the evitable and the inevitable, the foreseen and the unforeseen, the what-ifs and the emergencies. Then there are the events—the births of children, birthdays, holidays, graduations, weddings, education, vacations. Retirement, health care concerns, end-of-life issues, funeral planning, insurance protection—in our culture we do everything possible to make certain no stone is left unturned, that all the bases have been covered right up to death. But what about preparing for the next life?

The average life expectancy in my home state of Oregon is listed as seventy-nine years of age. Think about how much preparation is made for a physical life that may expire before the age of eighty.

And there is a major problem. None of those plans and preparations transfer into the next life. They have no value there.

This brings up a question. Since eternity is forever, wouldn't it be prudent to prepare for that life with the same measure of importance as we prepare for this earthly life? It seems it would be a good idea to make certain one is ready when it is time for that transition to be made. There is, after all, no turning back and no opportunity for a change of mind or a redo.

How *does* one prepare for eternity? While that question has, indeed, been raised, I do not have a go-to answer. There is no pamphlet or brochure that lists the steps and the process for that. The reason is because people cannot prepare themselves to meet God.

This much I know: The first step is the acknowledgment that God *exists* and that we need to be made ready for the next life, as that life will either continue with Him or without Him. There is nothing more we can do. The rest is in His hands. I also know He will not turn anyone away who comes to Him with a genuine desire and a pure heart. All it takes is a simple request.

Being prepared and living in the knowledge of that preparation is a gift, a treasure. Not a single one of us knows when this physical life is coming to an end. So, in my thinking, time is always of the essence. I would never want to enter eternity with regret.

Why do I ask you to consider this matter? Because eternity is a long, long time, and each one of you matters.

> A man's life consisteth not in the abundance of the
> things which he possesseth. —Luke 12:15 (KJV)

> The ground of a certain rich man brought forth plentifully: "And I will say to my soul, Soul, thou hast much goods laid up for many years; take thine ease, eat, drink, and be merry. But God said unto him, Thou fool, this night thy soul shall be required of thee: then whose shall those things be, which thou hast provided? So is he that layeth up treasure for himself, and is not rich toward God."
> —Luke 12:16, 19–21 (KJV)

On Eternity

eternity: n. Existence without end, infinite time.

I believe in eternity, a time without end that we enter into upon leaving this earth. Not everyone believes this. I was once shown a time line. Imagine a line that goes as far as the eye can see from east to west. Imagine also a sliver touching that line. That is how much time life upon this planet shares in the whole scope of time. Minuscule is not an adequate description.

When I was a little girl, I would strain my brain as though it was a muscle I could flex, trying with all my might to envision eternity. How can there be time without end? It is beyond the comprehension of our finite minds regardless of one's age.

As I grew older, I found myself questioning the reason for things such as pain, suffering, heartache, circumstances beyond anyone's control. We all have our own lists, and we also have more questions than answers, with zero understanding.

When questioning my Creator about one such incident, I heard in my mind, *Eternity is a long, long time.* In that one comment, I understood—though to a very limited degree—but I did understand.

God is a God of love. Contrary to the publicity waged against Him, He does not have a single cruel bone in His being. His main desire is to have a relationship with us, His children. When difficult situations occur in life, we make the choice of either turning to Him, on Him, or away from Him. He doesn't gain pleasure when our lives become difficult. He does want to be given the chance to be part of our stories.

We human beings are stubborn, self-sufficient, independent creatures bent on destruction. When we continue on in our own merry way and ignore Him, His choices become limited. He will do His best to get the attention of His children since there are no second chances once we have passed over.

In reality, He is the innovator of tough love. All that He does comes from that base of love. He cares and never wants any of us to have to deal with the reality of waiting until it is too late.

While returning from work today, I found myself thinking about my writing. So much of what I lay out has a spiritual emphasis. That is where and how I live my life, and my life is what I share. Contemplating the gravity of the subject matter, I wondered, *Should I try to lighten the content, make it more appealing?* Once again, I thought, *Eternity is a long, long time.* The focus of the writing won't change. It can't, because it is my calling. It is my life.

My challenge to you is as follows: The next time you are faced with a difficult situation in your life, one that brings the onslaught of questions and doubts, consider it in the light of eternity. Ask for truth and for understanding. You may be surprised. Are you going to have all the answers to everything? No, you won't! But you might just see things from a point of view you've never had before.

If any one of you do this, then I have done my job of opening a door and pointing the way to God.

How long is eternity? Eternity is a long, long time.

> Ask, and it will be given you; search, and you will find; knock, and the door will be opened for you.
> —Matthew 7:7